"*You alone are limited nowhere. You can choose to be whatever you decide to be, according to your own will. Not heavenly, not earthly, not mortal, not immortal did I create you. For you yourself shall be your own master and builder and creator according to your own will and your own honour. So you are free to sink to the lowest level of the animal kingdom but you may also soar into the highest spheres of creation.*"

Pico Della Mirandola (1463 – 1494)
Italian Renaissance Philosopher
Oration on the Dignity of Man

Order this book online at www.trafford.com/05-3157
or email orders@trafford.com

Most Trafford titles are also available at major online book retailers.

Note for Librarians: A cataloguing record for this book is available from Library
and Archives Canada at www.collectionscanada.ca/amicus/index-e.html

Printed in Victoria, BC, Canada.

ISBN: 978-1-4120-8191-7 (Trafford Edition)

ISBN 0-9738509-0-6 (I.C.D Edition)

I.C.D PUBLISHING COMPANY, c/o York Learning Academy Inc,
45 Sheppard Avenue East,
North York, Ontario, Canada M2N 5W9 (I.C.D edition)

 www.trafford.com

North America & international
toll-free: 1 888 232 4444 (USA & Canada)
phone: 250 383 6864 ♦ fax: 250 383 6804 ♦ email: info@trafford.com

The United Kingdom & Europe
phone: +44 (0)1865 722 113 ♦ local rate: 0845 230 9601
facsimile: +44 (0)1865 722 868 ♦ email: info.uk@trafford.com

10 9 8 7 6 5 4 3

GEOFFREY SMITH

THE ART OF EFFECTIVE LIVING

The Theory and Practice of Vision Renaissance

TRAFFORD PUBLISHING
Victoria, BC, Canada
(Trafford Edition)

I.C.D PUBLISHING COMPANY
Toronto, Ont, Canada
(ICD Edition)

I.C.D
PUBLISHING

The "New Reality" Seminars

The "New Reality" seminars upon which this book is based are intensive, thought-provoking 4-day courses in self-understanding and personal development that provide a powerful tool for achieving a happy, effective and self-directed lifestyle. By a proven combination of talks, awareness exercises, small group discussion, meditation and self-administered and self-evaluated questionnaires you will learn how to:

– Strengthen your relationships –
– Develop your full potential –
– Change unwanted habits –
– Increase self-esteem –

The Renewal Network is an informal association of personal growth groups which meet regularly to continue the practical guidance of the "New Reality" seminars. Meeting in an atmosphere of fellowship and mutual understanding, the workshops and groups are designed for thoughtful people of all ages, backgrounds and religions who seek meaning to their lives, the means to create a truly self-directed existence and the company of similar people.

For full information on the "New Reality" seminars please visit:

www.newrealityseminars.ca

Email: admin@yorklearningco.ca

or phone:

905 – 886 – 4910

I dedicate this book to my son Nicholas and his wife Nancy, to my daughter Mandy and her husband Derek, to my wife Miriam and my grandchildren Sebastian, Bianca, Angelica and Victoria and for those who are to come. Thank you for giving meaning to my life.

For information about Geoff Smith's work, or the intensive
4-day "New Reality" seminars and retreats which are
based on this book, please contact him at:

New Reality Seminars
c/o The York Learning Academy Inc.
North York Square, 45 Sheppard Avenue East,
Suite 900, North York, Ontario, Canada M2N 5W9
Email: admin@yorklearningco.ca
Tele # 905 – 886 – 4910

Or please visit:

www.newrealityseminars.ca

Further copies of this book are available from
New Reality Seminars.

www.newrealityseminars.ca

THE ART OF EFFECTIVE LIVING

How can I be happy, how can I live effectively and what stops me from doing so? To a great degree and in many ways, all religions and philosophies have tried to answer these questions. The greatest thinkers of each respective age have tried to pass that wisdom on to their generation and to successive ones, orally and through the written word. From them we can learn how to live well, how to relate with the world around us and how, within its many constraints, to live a happy life.

Although the great ideas that these questions have nurtured have often differed in many areas, their answers have remained in remarkable agreement. For a practical application of this wisdom in a day-to-day setting, however, we are often obliged to turn from the high peaks of oral and written wisdom to the ordinary valleys of human endeavour.

The principles, conclusions and suggestions outlined in this book are not new. The author makes no claim to originality of thought, but only to the much lesser talent of interpreting past philosophies in a practical way. It is to the giants of our civilization - past, present and to come, whose wisdom has illuminated the human heart that credit is due.

Geoff Smith

Acknowledgements

"How much we owe to the labours of our brothers! Day by day
they dig far from the sun that we may be warm, enlist and fight
in outposts of peril that we may be secure and brave the terrors
of the unknown for truths that shed light on our way"
– Anonymous

In writing this book I am deeply indebted to the many wonderful people over the years who have inspired me by their wisdom, courage and compassion. Each of them, in their own way and by advice and example, have provided the framework from which I have constructed a life of meaning, experience and inspiration. There are too many to thank specifically by name, most of you know who you are however, and those who do not and who I have admired and loved from a distance will continue to remain unaware of my anonymous admiration.

For the practical purpose of publishing this book, however, I would like to specifically thank Tatiana Usachev and Catherine Muir for their comprehensive editorial skills and for often bringing me painfully down from the clouds to a more acceptable literary style.

I would also like to thank Bettina Bros, Derek Goring, Elena Kostina, Bill Curtis and Jennifer Miller for their wide-ranging and intensive reviews and comments, Margherita Cammarota, whose kindness is an inspiration and who also reviewed this book with perception and understanding, Eva Woroniecka, whose lust for life is awesome, Lesley Soden, who prodded me firmly but gently to stop talking about writing and to do it, Cliff Graham, a humble man whose calm endurance and professional ethics made him the best manager I ever had, my mother Lilian, a wonderful woman whose memory through the long years I continue to cherish and finally to my father Clifford, a kind and gentle man to whom I should have shown greater compassion and taken the time, patience and understanding to know better.

Contents

Part Two. The Practice of Vision Renaissance

Introduction

We consist of a few elements that have always existed but in each of us they have come together in a unique never to be repeated combination that has been gifted with life. As with all gifts, we should use it well and develop within us the ability to learn, love, care, create, harmonize and experience. The felt experience of this growth is happiness. We experience pain when it is absent, suppressed, reversed or limited.

Our feelings and actions are created by the way we rightly or wrongly interpret the realities of life and not by the events in our life to which we respond. This interpretation is based mainly on the feedback we received from our environment, family and culture. If the feedback was faulty or wrongly interpreted it will create inappropriate beliefs, emotions and subsequent actions that will then limit our ability to live effectively.

Beliefs that limit us can be isolated and changed to life-enhancing ones and then made a permanent part of our lifestyle by the process we call "Vision Renaissance."

A unique and totally personal picture of reality creates our thoughts, emotions and actions. It consists of a felt sense and memory of all our experiences, our interpretation of them and an opinion as to how to deal with them. In "Vision Renaissance" we call this picture our "vision." Although our "vision" is deeply held and strongly defended, there is often a painful gulf between our dreams and the ultimate reality that our vision produces. This gulf prevents us from living the full life that is both our birthright and obligation. In this book I will examine the reason for this gulf and how in a dynamic and practical way it can be bridged.

Most people only see a fraction of the beautiful things that pass daily in front of their eyes, they only hear a fraction of the music and poetry in the universe and only experience a few of the many emotions of which they are capable.

These emotions include love of others, and especially love of the most important person in their life, without which all personal growth is impossible, namely themselves.

Seeing these limitations, thoughtful men and woman ask why this is, and their search leads them to our great sources of wisdom including the Bible, Talmud, Koran, Dharmapada, the Vedantic tradition of India, the philosophies of Spinoza, Kant, Schopenauer, Socrates and Aristotle. Eventually they may pursue the works of the great psychologists, behaviourists and social thinkers of history. Eventually, however, and if their search is both diligent and patient, they will find that although all these great traditions differ substantially and often dramatically from one another, they are all in remarkable agreement in their answers to two questions. How can I be happy, and, what stops me? In this book I will elaborate upon the central theme of these traditional teachings and will show how they present a highly practical framework for living that can be effected immediately in your daily life.

In Part One, I will examine the development of your own unique "vision", the areas of it which hinder your growth and how it can be changed and made permanent. There is a Canadian Indian proverb, which states: "Man is born to suffering as the sparks fly upwards." While I certainly do not believe in the inevitability of suffering any more than an automatic entitlement to pleasure, I do believe that we all experience both joy and anguish and that the felt experience of these can be largely self-directed. This book is a guide to embracing the joy and facing the anguish.

In Part Two, I will apply the understanding of the development of your "vision" to the four major areas of its growth including how you see yourself, others, your world values and life itself. These directly affect one's self-esteem, relationships and experiences. A positive "vision" of self allows you to reach out to those around you. This then permits an effective relationship with those things in the world that are valued and finally with life itself. Abraham Maslow, in his wonderful book,

Towards a Psychology of Being, describes this integration of self, others, values and life as self-actualization and your belief system as a combination of these four areas.

This book is a serious and practical guide to the development of self-understanding and provides the means to construct a truly practical framework for an effective life. It is directed, and *only* directed, to serious students of living who are prepared to work at this process enthusiastically and with commitment and vigour. The text itself may in some instances have to be read more than once and the exercises involve a great deal of objective thought, a willingness to read the instructions thoroughly and the courage to relentlessly challenge existing patterns of thought and behaviour.

I recommend that you read this book from cover to cover and practise all the exercises. At the beginning of each chapter there are several important quotations from thinkers of both the past and present that you should read carefully and thoughtfully, as they are an integral part of the reading that follows. A very important part of this programme is the process of self-questioning which is generally outlined in the early part of each chapter. These questions are often in italics, as are significant parts of the text that are vitally important for you to understand. *Please do not skip the quotations, the self-directed questions or the emphasized italics, as their purpose is to encourage a self-awareness that is imperative if full benefit from the book is to be obtained.*

The first part is mainly theoretical and you may be tempted to skip it and move to Part Two. It is important for me to tell you, however, that but for a deeply committed belief in the theoretical principles of Part One and the developing process by which they lead to their effective practice in Part Two, the book would never have been written in the first place.

Geoffrey A. Smith
Thornhill, Ontario,
Canada
February 2006

Chapter One

MAJOR ASSUMPTIONS OF VISION RENAISSANCE

"The greatest revolution in our generation is the discovery that human beings, by changing the inner aspect of their mind, can change the outer aspect of their life."
William James

"Let a man strive to purify his thoughts. What a man thinketh, that is he; this is the eternal mystery. Dwelling within his Self with thoughts serene, he will obtain imperishable happiness. Man becomes that of which he thinks."
The Upanishads. Vedantic tradition of India

"A man is what he thinks about all day long."
Ralph Waldo Emerson

"A man's life is what his thoughts make of him."
Marcus Aurelias

"We do not see things as they are but as we are. Every person will be called to account on the day of judgement for the permitted pleasures in life that they failed to enjoy."
The Talmud

"You are today where your thoughts have brought you; you will be tomorrow where your thoughts take you."
James Allen

How can you live a full, happy and effective life in a complex modern world? How can you, as an authentic individual, passionately enjoy and experience this precious gift of life in a world of challenge, adversity, unreasonable expectations and unforeseen events? The search for the answers to these questions has persisted down through the long corridors of time. It is soon discovered that riches can quickly vanish and that fame, honour, power and success are frequently illusions. It is not surprising therefore that the search for this elusive bluebird has become our supreme quest and the cause of our hope. Philosophers have thought about it, psychologists have analysed it and poets have dreamed of it, but in this challenging book I am not concerned with the abstract thoughts of philosophy, the cold ruminations of science or the often escapist platitudes of dreamers, but instead with the practical answer to the question: How can I be a happy, authentic and genuine individual and what stops me? The simple answer is that your ability to be happy is fully and solely determined by the way you see and interpret the world about you (your vision) and you can change it. If you think the same thoughts frequently enough, they will develop into an "attitude" of mind and this belief will then become part of your vision of life. Subsequent events and your reactions to them will then be automatically directed by this belief rather than by the event, *even though it may be based upon a false, harmful or out-of-date interpretation of reality*. When this occurs the resulting emotions and actions will be inappropriate to your growth and may cause you to lead a crippled and stunted life. False "attitudes" can be recognized, isolated and changed by the process called "Vision Renaissance."

The mission of this book is to show how your vision can be accessed, understood and if needed changed so that happiness becomes your birthright rather than an illusion.

Many years ago a physician addressed a group of people on the dangerous effects of drinking too much alcohol. To demonstrate, she dropped an earthworm into a glass of water and watched as it swam to the side. She then placed it in the glass of alcohol whereupon it disintegrated. *"What is the moral of this?"* she asked quietly and after a few moments silence a slurred voice at the back of the room said, *"Well Doctor, the moral is obvious, if you booze, you sure won't get worms."* Although the story may be anecdotal it clearly identifies the major principle that flows through this book: *You do not see things as they are but as you choose to see them.*

It is this unique way that individuals choose to see and interpret an event that influences every aspect of their lives. It is this picture that they have of themselves, other people, their world and of life that directs their emotions and the actions that those emotions empower. In Vision Renaissance this is called one's *"Vision."* It is your *"Vision"* of reality that is fully responsible for your joy, enthusiasm and success and equally for your pain, frustration and anguish and not the events or circumstances that happen to you. These events only achieve meaning when you interpret them and the situation that surrounds them. *That interpretation may be faulty and life-diminishing and based on an incorrect interpretation of reality.* A simple example explains this principle.

If a group of people were asked to describe the meaning of the *second* symbol in each of the following sets of symbols:

D O G   2 O 3

They would generally identify them as the letter "O" (the vowel) in the first instance and zero (the number) in the second. The middle symbol in each example is of course the same. The "O" in the middle of each is a reality or a "given" over which you have no direct control but its meaning depends on your interpretation of the symbols around it (its environment) and can generally only be changed when you change that interpretation (i.e. from numbers to letters or the reverse). What is the significance of this in your daily life?

Your life is also governed by many factors over which you often have limited control. Your genetic makeup, race, physical constitution, cultural inheritance and social and economic environment are all the "givens" of your personal reality and as such can rarely be changed. These realities extend to more intrusive ones such as a difficult boss, unpleasant individuals, limited opportunities for growth, aging and financial resources. These factors or circumstances are generally beyond your immediate control but your freedom to interpret their meaning is almost totally within it. It is this freedom that is at the heart of the Vision Renaissance programme.

Each person has an internal and subconscious dialogue, which *justifies* their actions *no matter how limiting those actions may be*. It is *very* important that you understand this. *Your thoughts fully justify your subsequent actions, no matter how limiting or destructive those actions may be.* This self-talk is based on previously constructed beliefs and is the product of the social, parental and environmental influences that inform you about your world. It tells you how to act in response to an event and *suggests the consequences of not acting*. For example, repeated directions to be careful *every* time a growing child leaves the house, instead of a more generally suggested caution, will create an internalized dialogue based on the belief that the world outside is both the enemy and is dangerous.

"The world outside my immediate security is a source of great danger and I must avoid it and its experiences as much as possible OR ELSE I will be in great danger."

Constant criticism by parents, teachers or friends will create a dialogue based on personal inadequacy.

"I must be approved by everyone who is significant to me OR ELSE I will have no value."

Frequent compliments from an *otherwise* cold and unresponsive parent, when a child or young adult is useful or smart will create a dialogue based on conditional love.

"I must be useful OR ELSE I will not be lovable."

In the above examples, the internal self-talk is an *interpretation* of part of the individual's reality based upon their previous experience of it. They refer to the world, self-value and a personal capacity to be loved respectively. In Vision Renaissance this internal dialogue is referred to as an "attitude." Even though this belief may be incorrect and based upon a faulty interpretation of reality, it is this, *and not the event itself,* that creates and justifies the subsequent emotion and resultant action. It follows that if your emotions and actions or the results that follow from those actions are not appropriate to your happiness, success or growth, it is the belief creating them that should be changed. *The stimulating event is what you are given in life, the attitude is how you interpret that event and your emotions and actions follow directly from this belief.* You will note that this internalized interpretation tells you how to act in response to an event and suggests the consequences of not acting *(OR ELSE in the previous examples).* This is the basis of the Vision Renaissance programme which shows in a practical and dynamic way how inappropriate beliefs can be isolated, identified and changed. With this in mind the major principles of Vision Renaissance can now be stated.

"Every individual has a highly personal vision of life which consists of countless beliefs which evaluate every area of their reality. It is these beliefs that control their feelings and subsequent actions and not the original situation or stimulating event to which the action responds. In "Vision Renaissance" this highly unique personal picture of the world is called your "Vision" and the individual evaluations within it, your "Attitudes."

These attitudes or beliefs were developed from the cumulative interpretation of information received from parents, relatives, friends, culture and religion within the environment of growth.

"Attitudes" which have been created by faulty interpretations of reality will inevitably produce inappropriate emotions and actions which will limit the individual's ability to live effectively.

These attitudes, many of which can be toxic and life-limiting, can be isolated and changed to life-enhancing ones and these changes made a permanent part of a lifestyle and of a new "vision."

In this book the process of identification, reconstruction and change is called "Vision Renaissance."

Our personal vision may be described as a kind of jury box in which there are sitting thousands of jurors (Attitudes) each of whom are responsible for evaluating a particular area of our reality. When a particular situation arises the juror most responsible for evaluating it steps forward, claims the case as theirs and dictates an "appropriate" response.

There are four major developing areas of your "Vision" that I will be looking at in Vision Renaissance. These are: how you see yourself, how you see the people around you, how you see the world and finally how you see life.

Some of the most frequently held life-diminishing "Attitudes" are listed below. Please take a quiet moment and read through the list slowly and objectively several times. Ask yourself whether any of them are relevant in some way to YOUR beliefs or whether they influence part of YOUR life. *If there are, remember that each of them is irrational and damaging to your growth.*

(1) I have to please and be approved by people who are significant to me *OR ELSE* I will have no value.

(2) My decisions must be correct *OR ELSE* I will be a failure.

(3) As most people only care about themselves, I must put myself first in every situation O*R ELSE* I will miss out on life's opportunities.

(4) Life must be fair and just *OR ELSE* I will feel unjustly treated.

(5) My life must work out just how I planned *OR ELSE* it will be terrible and I will be unhappy.

(6) I must have talent, competence, success or recognition in at least one area of my life *OR ELSE* I will be a failure.

(7) As God is an all powerful tyrant, I must obey all his laws *OR ELSE* he will withdraw his love and punish me.

(8) I must be useful to those I love *OR ELSE* I will not be lovable.

(9) I must keep myself productively busy most of the time *OR ELSE* I will feel like I am wasting my time and/or being useless.

I will be discussing specific aspects of your vision, how (if needed) they can be changed and their impact on an effective life in later chapters but first, the following critical questions need to be answered:

· What are the major conflicts that prevent the achieving of an effective life?

· What is the "authentic self" that one needs in order to live effectively and how does it function?

· What are the major elements and needs of an "authentic self?"

· Why is the development of an "authentic self" an important aspect of an effective life?

1. MAJOR CONFLICTS

It is only within the security of an effective life that you can march forward into the fullness of life. For many people, however, there is a significant gulf between their hopes and the reality upon which those hopes are based. It is this gulf that causes their pain and that prevents them from living effectively in terms of what they achieve, feel and do. This frequently results in non-achievement, non-feeling and non-action.

It is the resolution of these conflicting areas of hopes, dreams and reality that provides the fertile ground in which the development of an effective life can begin. It seems that often there are two conflicting forces pulling people in opposite directions. For these to be brought together, it is important to understand their attraction, significance and limitations. These conflicting pressures can be described as *cultural conformity* and the desire for an *authentic self.*

Cultural Conformity

On one side, there is that part of your biological personality that obliges you to conform to your environment, culture, race, religion, gender, country and class. Each of these has expectations and makes demands upon you. Sometimes these demands are expressed in a subtle manner and are imposed in a restrained way. At other times they are enforced by more rigidly applied religious or social dogma, but either way they constantly challenge an individual's need for self-expression, freedom and growth. These expectations are not in themselves sinister or dangerous, in fact, the reverse is true as they are a necessary part of human survival.

It is only when a rigidly imposed adherence to these norms conflicts with freedom and individual human growth within the acceptable limits of social structure, that cultural conformity should be viewed with caution, and if necessary challenged or overruled.

Nature and the biological forces that control us are primarily involved in our survival, not in the finer qualities of personal growth or how we experience and explore the gift of life. There are two powerful tools that come into play to achieve this. The first of these is fear and the second is a need to conform. Fear creates caution and a desire to retreat to a position of security. Information is then gathered, the danger interpreted and evaluated and an appropriate course of action decided upon. It is within that zone of security that a sub-group, group or tribe is formed. The process of retreat is assisted by the second of nature's imperatives, conformity. The need to conform is biologically self-imposed but it is also a condition of membership in the group. The result of this is an initial and deeply felt need to be the same as those around us coupled with a social obligation to do so. Full personal growth can only be achieved when these needs and obligations are recognized, challenged, integrated and when needed, overcome.

Your individual security lies in not standing above or outside of the group and in conforming to its standards. The security of the *group* lies in your conforming to its rules.

Although the two imperatives of fear and conformity achieve their survival aims, they frequently challenge an individual's development towards an effective life. In fact they often seriously conflict with it, in that *the fear and conformity that protects you and your group are the same ones that can impede your growth.*

An Authentic Self

The need for cultural conformity frequently conflicts with the development of an authentic self. But what is "an authentic self?" Are we deluding ourselves in believing that one exists? Are we not machines that function, break and are eventually discarded depending upon the variables of our construction and use? If we are something more, what are we? What are our obligations to that "something" and how can we fulfil those obligations? Finally, are there specific and practical steps that can be taken to develop and enhance that authenticity?

It is vital that these questions be answered in order for a framework for an effective life to be developed. If they are not answered, or if an authentic self is a delusion, the quest for an effective life as an expression of that authenticity becomes meaningless.

The Oxford dictionary defines authentic as referring to something that is *"based on facts and is genuine and accurate."*

It originates from the Greek word *"authentikos"* meaning genuine.

The question, "Do you have an individually recognizable self?" has haunted and eluded philosophers, theologians and scientists since time immemorial. Every suggested answer takes the questioner deeper into the original dilemma.

It can be said for example that the "self" is the initiator of action but machines cannot start themselves and although the path of an action can be physically measured, the initial thought and how it implements action cannot. Other approaches suggest that the "self" is either that which is aware of itself or merely a process that interprets and internalizes external information, but both of these fail to answer the question who or what does this and how is the information physically recorded as a guide to future behaviour. Biology suggests that awareness of self is purely a physical function of the brain but this implies that all animals are self-aware which is a postulate that is disputed.

Psychologists in their understandable eagerness to construct a satisfactory model of the "self" have suggested that it is nothing more than a flexible psychological framework that internalizes reality, supports awareness and places a value upon that of which we have become aware. It is felt that the major progressive factors that influence the development of this framework are *initial trust, personal nurture, autonomy, identification and social intimacy,* all of which will be discussed in detail later in this chapter. Finally theology suggests that the "self" is spiritual, eternal and connected with the divine.

What is not in dispute is that it exists. Of greater relevance however is not what an authentic self is, so much as its purpose and the practical steps needed to ensure that it is developed as the core of an effective life.

2. FUNCTIONS OF THE "SELF"

- The "self" operates as a filter through which external events are internalized, interpreted, given meaning, recorded and then developed into personality trends and future tendencies.

- It is flexible and self-protective, often projecting a public image that is different from that which is felt.

- It is reflective and observes itself acting as a filter.

- It is the *initiating* organizer of thoughts, feelings, motives, actions and observations.

- It integrates those thoughts, feelings, motives, actions and observations into a whole that becomes a felt sense of identity, aspects of which are then externalized.

- It coordinates that experience in time to produce a sense of continuity, constancy and predictability.

It may be argued that the above broadly-based description of the major functions of the "self" ignores some of the fundamental issues of what, who and where. This is a valid comment, but it does capture what is currently known, based on decades of scientific research and spiritual observation. What is really important is the impact that these functions have on the development of an effective life.

3. DEVELOPING ELEMENTS OF AN AUTHENTIC SELF

As mentioned earlier, the fertile ground in which authenticity is gradually developed consists of five elements: (a) Trust (b) Personal Nurture (c) Autonomy (d) Identity and (e) Social Intimacy. The following describes those elements in order of their developmental importance.

(a) Trust

Your ability to trust starts early in life and in its initial stages depends almost exclusively on how you are received into the world. The signs that you see, hear and feel indicate to you the degree of your acceptance in the world and you then learn which areas of it are "safe." That feeling of safety is related to the people around you and the environment they produce. You then begin to develop trust and self-reliance in your own ability to make appropriate choices within that secure environment.

(b) Personal Nurture

The developing knowledge that you can make realistic and successful choices about your safety, security and comfort is a vital part of your growth. It allows you to trust your survival decisions and to widen that process. This includes the less tangible but vitally important area of self-love. You care for those who you trust to look after you with confidence and that affection naturally extends to yourself, if you are indeed the confident caregiver. *It is this developing confidence in your own decision-making ability and the trust and personal affection that naturally stems from it that creates, develops and then maintains authenticity.*

(c) Autonomy

This growing confidence and trust in your ability to make appropriate survival decisions then allows you to slowly reduce your initial dependencies while developing a realistic and autonomous self-identity. At the same time, and because the process of leaving those dependencies behind is a gradual one, your own skills are seen as additional to your original sources of comfort rather than "rebellious" substitutes for them. This maintains the essential balance between personal autonomy *(authentic self)* and social integration *(cultural conformity).*

(d) Identity

Your growing independence identifies with ever-increasing clarity who you are and what you are becoming. This picture is a flexible collage of your felt and internalized needs, aspirations and fears and a growing confidence in your own ability to deal with them.

At the same time as this picture is forming, however, there is a growing awareness that this independence is closely related to and dependent upon your social environment for its maintenance. This awareness suggests to you that although you are separate from your social group you are in many ways dependent upon it, *not only for practical survival but also for the development and maintenance of your identity in the first place*. This awareness leads to a need for various aspects and levels of social intimacy. You then become a fully functional social being, the awareness of which forms the structured core of your identity.

(e) Social Intimacy

The internalized pressure to maintain a strongly developing sense of who you are does not wane as it is realized; on the contrary, it becomes more intense and insistent. At the same time it becomes increasingly evident that one of the major factors in your personal development and its maintenance is the interaction between your internalized sense of self and those around you. It becomes obvious that your self-identity is dependent on, influenced by and in many ways created by your social interaction with others. Your growing uniqueness and independence often produces a sense of isolation and it is within the anguish of that isolation and the knowledge of your identity's dependence upon others that you need and reach out for connection, closeness, intimacy and eventually love whilst at the same time always struggling to maintain your own separate identity.

A truly authentic "self" will grow and reach fullness only in the soil of initial trust and acceptance. In its earliest stages this creates a growing confidence that reliable survival deci-sions can be made. When these survival and caring decisions are successful a growing independence is developed along with affection and trust for the "self" who is making those decisions. That combination of self-trust and self-affection develops a positive, clear and viable self-image, which then demands inti-mate social relations as a fundamental condition of continuing growth. *If this growth, or the soil in which it occurs is deficient, there will be limited authenticity, and you will not move forward into the fullness of life. You will exist but you will not live effec-tively.*

4. IMPORTANCE OF AN AUTHENTIC SELF

Part of your identity is a result of genetic and ancestral make-up because your appearance, health, physical body, intelligence, and some personality tendencies are generally inherited from your forebears. The importance of these in determining your personality and the life you lead is, however, a matter of signifi-cant discussion and dispute. This is because it is also apparent that environment plays a significant role in your growth. An individual's growth environment is a combination of religious, cultural, gender, social and childhood influence and input. The interdependence of nature versus nurture is an important one as it directly affects the extent to which individual effort can bring about constructive change. To appreciate this dependen-cy you have to look at the interaction between your inherited nature and social influence from the viewpoint of an *ongoing* and interdependent process of cause and effect.

As a starting point, it is reasonable to suggest that nothing exists that was not created. Individuality or consciousness of "self" is created by a subtle interplay of cause and effect between inherited nature and environment. Even in your early stages of growth you are a developing product of both. As an identifiable "self" begins to grow, it projects itself onto its environment, and then observes the feedback from it. This input validates, fails to validate or invalidates completely the growing self-image and the picture is adjusted accordingly.

Hidden within this continuous interplay of personal tendencies and adjustment to environmental feedback is an awareness of the process itself. It is the observer of this process who is identified as the "self" and who ultimately determines what is projected, how that projection is made and *how the feedback is interpreted.*

If the "self" that is being developed and then projected is genuine and truly represents an honest projection of the individual's needs, aspirations, trust, feelings and conclusions, the feedback received will reinforce that reality. If it is not authentic, the feedback will, *by the same process,* reinforce the pretence and create an illusion. This illusion will be accepted even if it restricts the development of a truly effective life.

In this book the process of developing, maintaining and projecting our authenticity and its subsequent validation by feedback is referred to as the process of "Self-affirmation." The retelling of a simple Grimm's fairy tale can demonstrate the magic of this process.

One day a beautiful princess called Rapunzel was captured by an ugly, straggly-haired, wart-covered old witch and taken by her to the turret of a secret castle as a prisoner. The witch did not lock Rapunzel in her room but instead took all the mirrors in the castle away and every day told Rapunzel that she was ugly and not fit to be in the outside world. Rapunzel believed her of course, as she had no way to prove otherwise and thus became a prisoner, not of the witch, but of her own imagined ugliness.

Some time later a handsome prince galloped by and looked up. Seeing this beautiful but lonely maiden looking out of her window, he climbed down from his horse and smiled. She smiled in return, and thus encouraged, he climbed up to see her. When he did so and she saw reflected in the glistening part of his eyes the fact that she was beautiful, she was free from her self-imposed chains.

The story concludes as all great stories do, with a happy ending. The Prince rescues the Princess and they gallop off into the sunset, get married and live happily ever after. You may ask why the Princess believed the positive feedback of the Prince over the negative feedback of the Witch. This apparent conflict will be discussed in greater detail later. It is sufficient for the moment, however, to say that in everyone there is a psychologically-based urge towards growth, wholeness and freedom that is an extension of our more basic survival instinct and complements it. We search for those experiences and people that may assist us in fulfilling that demand. We may never find them, but it is the belief that we will that provides the foundation for all human hope and it this inborn "tendency to wholeness" that is the basis of our growth.

The message in this beautiful little story is that the clever witch realized that if she put locks on the door, the princess would always want to be free. By taking away the mirrors the witch ensured that Rapunzel became her own guard and a prisoner of her own imagination. A further example will widen this observation.

In a travelling circus one might wonder how several performing elephants are kept captive, considering their tremendous strength. It would seem that at each new venue they would *each* have to be confined by a heavy chain in a large pre-concreted pit. In reality however, a newly arrived baby elephant is simply tethered to the ground with a stick and a piece of string. It tries to escape, realizes it is tethered *and never forgets*. Ten years later, although it is now a seven-ton adult it still remains, like Rapunzel, a prisoner of its own *imagined limits,* when all it would have to do to regain its freedom is to nod its head.

When the Prince stood in front of Rapunzel, he was in essence saying, "I see you, I understand you, you are beautiful and I love you", and it was this unconditional affirmation that freed her from her imagined limitations. All of us are in our own way prisoners of our own *perceived boundaries*. Through the process of Vision Renaissance these boundaries can be recognized and eliminated.

SUMMARY OF CHAPTER ONE

1.   The life of every individual is controlled by a unique picture (Vision) of the world, which directs their emotions and actions.

2.   An effective life can only be achieved when the conflict between an individual's cultural identity and their need for an authentic self are fully reconciled within this Vision.

3.   An authentic self is the product of a developing combination of trust, personal nurture, autonomy, developing identity and social intimacy.

4.   The unique Vision of life that every individual holds is made up of many beliefs which evaluate their reality, control their emotions and direct their actions. In this book these beliefs are referred to as "Attitudes."

5.   These "Attitudes" are formed from the input that is received by the individual from the world around them (parents, family, friends, culture and faith).

6.   These "Attitudes" may be incorrect or inappropriate interpretations of reality and as such will create emotions and actions that are inappropriate to a fully effective life.

7.   Inappropriate and life-limiting "Attitudes" can be isolated and changed and those changes can be made a permanent part of a new Vision. In this book this process of proactive change is referred to as "Vision Renaissance."

Chapter Two

AN EFFECTIVE LIFE

"Every year that I live, I am more convinced that the waste of life lies in the love we have not given, the powers we have not used or developed and in the selfish caution which risking nothing in its avoidance of pain, misses any chance at happiness."
John B. Tabb

"The art of living successfully consists of being able to hold two opposite ideas in tension at the same time. To make long-term plans as if you were going to live forever and to conduct your daily life as if you were going to die tomorrow."
Sydney J. Harris

"The opposite of courage in our society is not cowardice – it's conformity."
Rollo May

"The problem is not that so many of us fail at living, but that most of us never bother to try it."
G. K. Chesterton

"The past, present and future are fluid components of your life and eternally flow through it. The past is the context which will guide tomorrow's mission and the present is your field of action. The question to be asked is: What is your mission and how will today's actions achieve it?"
The Author

The specific process by which your "Vision" is formed, dissected and if needed, changed, is covered in the following chapters but two important questions need to be answered first.

(a) What is an effective life?

(b) What are the universal values that should govern it?

Ultimately, individuals must decide for themselves what they see as an effective life, as this is a unique collage of their own values, needs and ideals. As a guide to beginning the process of Vision Renaissance, however, I would suggest the following definition:

> *"The Effective Life is lived with a passionate belief that it is worthwhile. It is lived with a self-induced enthusiasm, an appetite for living and with an all-transforming determination to savour life to the full.*
>
> *It tastes the sweets of existence and as it progressively achieves its own worthy ideals, lives vigorously and to the limits of its physical, mental and spiritual capacities."*

Within this broadly-based definition I believe it is possible to construct a framework upon which an effective life is built. There are nine components of this framework:

(a) *Trust your judgement*

(b) *Be patient and make a friend of time*

(c) *Practise a gentle humility*

(d) *Be led by your reason*

(e) *Face life with fortitude*

(f) *Give life a chance and take a risk*

(g) *Practise self-love*

(h)   Be interested and be interesting

(i)   Dare to dream and dare to act

Let us look at each of these in detail.

(a) Trust Your Judgement

Your opinions, standards of performance, ethics and values reflect who you are and are the result of the unique journey that you have taken. When these are expressed, defended and maintained, they strengthen your confidence and ability to enrich your identity. Enlightened self-interest and basic courtesy, however, oblige you to do so with patience and respect for the opinions of others. They have also travelled their own unique path and are expressing *their* truth in the same way that you are expressing yours. An individually-felt identity is developed, however, by the presentation of *your* truth and a reasoned evaluation of theirs. Maintaining and proclaiming your standards, values and ethics implies that you have a clearly understood perception of what they are in the first place. This perception is then maintained and reinforced by the actions you take to proclaim and defend them. These actions include a desire to develop or to reduce in yourself those qualities you admire or dislike in others and a reluctance to lower your standards to compete at the level of those who challenge you.

Maintaining your own standards requires you to recognize the weaknesses of others, the strengths in yourself and the *social obligation* that these differences involve. It requires you to follow an internally felt *"noblesse oblige"* that obliges you to use your strengths and talents for the benefit and growth of those who are weaker or less skilled.

In defending your own beliefs, it is important to remember that the popularity of an opinion does not confer upon it a greater truth, wisdom or validity. Indeed the reverse is often true, in that many popular beliefs, backed as they often are by emotional needs rather than reason, offer a safe haven for those individuals who wish to escape from the burden of thinking and of personal responsibility.

Strongly influencing this obligation to proclaim your own beliefs is the need to be open-minded and flexible. It has often been said that strong characters have the courage of their convictions, but unfortunately, every tyrant in history and their followers have had this, and this in itself is no guarantee of wisdom. What is of greater importance is to have the courage and open-minded flexibility to reject convictions when they don't match up with reality or logic. This open-minded attitude to truth does not mean avoiding giving an opinion, or failing to defend one, but it does imply an obligation to search for new information in its pursuit.

(b) Be Patient and Make a Friend of Time

Patience is an important part of an effective lifestyle. The ability to forgo the need for instant results and gratification is a defining characteristic of the effective individual. It is a vitally important part of their growth in that it reconciles and integrates their intellect, intuition and desire.

All life forms are governed by survival instincts that operate at an emotional level. Human life forms are additionally equipped with an intellect that allows them to plan for longer, more durable, and more effective ways of ensuring survival. In many individuals however, this longer-term reasoning capacity is often overruled by their immediate emotional needs and when it is, they lose the essential quality that makes them human.

We see examples of this in every area of our society and it has been so strongly built into our lives that our economy relies on it. High prices are paid to ensure immediate delivery instead of more cautious shopping, luxury products can be purchased with no deposit, creating the illusion of instant wealth, interest rates finance immediate purchases in preference to saving, fast food is consumed instead of a more patiently prepared and nutritious diet, short-term relaxation is usually chosen over the longer-term benefits of exercise, instant entertainment has replaced the longer-term benefits of study and work, the information highway has replaced the "felt" knowledge of tedious research and the deeply-thought wisdom of appropriate lifestyle management has been replaced by the instantly absorbed "self help" cliché. Indeed, inflation itself seductively builds into our economy the concept of *automatic* rising prices and the illusion of *increased wealth* by mortgaging the economic security of future generations.

The list is endless. In each of these examples the same dynamic is at work and the survival question, *"What can you do to feel good immediately?"* has been answered. Motivated by these emotional needs and the opportunity for immediate satisfaction, reason takes a back seat and long-term benefits are ignored.

It is important to realize that it is not the pleasures of taste, entertainment, relaxation or the purchase of desired goods that is the problem here, but the immediate gratification that they will provide versus the greater pleasure that can often be achieved by rational delay.

What individuals who put gratification first frequently overlook is that the immediate pleasure is often reduced by the knowledge that a price has to be paid later for the current indulgence. Individuals who delay gratification have no such fear as the price has already been paid in advance and the pleasure has been justified and earned.

Our present society is almost totally based on the encouragement of early satisfaction. Faced with this, is it not surprising that so many individuals believe in their right and obligation to enjoy now and pay later? This is, however, a belief that weakens human character.

Why is it that some individuals are motivated by the need for instant gratification far more than others? No one really knows of course but it is known that the development of this tendency, as with many others, is strongly influenced by attitudes learned from our culture and social environment. These seriously impact on the inherent tendencies with which we are born.

As mentioned earlier, there is an internalized process of "self-talk" which justifies an individual's actions *no matter how limiting those actions may be.* This self-talk is a product of the social and parental influences that inform individuals about their world. In later chapters I will show how "Vision Renaissance" can change these messages.

Inherent in the need for immediate benefit is the implication that time is limited and that as there isn't much of it, it should somehow be controlled. This creates insecurity and a lack of endurance.

The effective individual realizes, however, that time cannot be controlled and that the real beauty and understanding of life can only be experienced through the filter of patient observation. We can be the beneficiaries of time or its victims but we can never be its master.

In describing this need for patient observation of the mysteries of life, a great rabbi once asked a man who was in a very great hurry why he rushed so much. *"I am in pursuit of life and its experiences,"* he replied breathlessly. *"And why are you so sure that life runs ahead of you?"* replied the rabbi. *"Maybe it lies behind you, and you need to pause until it catches up."*

True patience is a form of personal courage, which is actively expressed by perseverance. True perseverance, which is the spiritual equivalent of action, is one of the strongest forces in the world and is almost unbeatable. Talent, genius or intellect can rarely compete with or overtake persistence and it is often only this that can carry you to the summits so aptly described by the English poet Longfellow:

> *"The heights that great men reached and kept*
> *Were not attained by sudden flight,*
> *But they, while their companions slept,*
> *Were toiling upward in the night."*

It is said that time is the great healer of human misfortune and the bearer of its greatest joy. It is therefore imperative that you make an ally of time and allow its magic to work to your benefit. Patience will make a friend of time, while impatience will always make it your enemy.

(c) Practise a Gentle Humility and Esteem Others

In an assessment of personal character, a frequent mistake is the assumption that gentleness and humility are indicators of personal weakness. As a general rule, nothing could be further from the truth. This error is similar to the belief that genuine self-love is a form of selfishness, when in fact it is on the opposite end of the self-development spectrum.

While open expressions of strength are often coarse expressions of weakness, *genuine* gentleness and humility are usually the subtlest expressions of personal strength. They are often expressed by individuals who are secure enough within their own boundaries to release others from protecting theirs. The words and actions of the gentle man or woman say, *"You need not fear me, for when you are with me I will make you secure enough to be who you are and to feel what you wish to feel."* It is within this secure and fertile field that another person's self-love, confidence and esteem can grow and flourish, fertilized by the freedom to grow that your actions will have conferred upon them. Persons who practise a gentle humility and who esteem others lead and guide by example rather than by coercion and in doing so improve the world around them. These individuals realize that overt expressions of strength and arrogance repress the spirit and character of others and invariably lead to resentment and opposing displays of strength.

Strong individuals who practise gentle humility do not doubt their powers, but in the subtlest of ways, proclaim them. They believe that whatever strength, skill or talent they may have is not possessed *by* them, but operates *through* them. They feel a moral obligation to use those abilities wisely and cautiously for the benefit, protection and uplifting of others who may not be as strong.

When you practise genuine humility you search for the positive qualities in others and make appreciative comments such as, *"That was really kind of you"*, *"How nice of you to - - -"*, *"Thank you so much for - - -"*, and evaluative ones like *"Well done, you really did well when you - - -"*, *"You are really good at - - -."* No human being is without some, and generally many, redeeming features and as long as you are aware of the need to find them, you will do so. The esteem that you give to others must, however, be sincere. Human intuition is almost infallible and if you are merely trying to encourage someone to say nice things about you in return or to hook them in some way, they will know it and will quickly reject you. You must *genuinely* want the other person to like and value themselves and to see their positive qualities and your affirmation of these qualities must be a reflection of that sincerity. It is only in an atmosphere of genuine and mutual acceptance that a truly honest relationship can grow.

In my Art of Effective Living classes when people know each other a little, they are asked to describe at least one positive quality about everyone else. This results in a magical increase in the warmth, dynamism and energy of the working groups.

Genuine humility should not be confused with a falsely-proclaimed servility that is quickly recognized as crude manipulation. The major characteristics of those who manipulate by servile flattery and those who do not are described below:

Authenticity and Humility	*Manipulation*
Affirms and defends own values	*Negates or denies own values*
Values do not depend upon social or personal gain	*Values depend upon personal gain and approval of others*
Accepts the unconditional right and value of own existence	*Deny their own rights in favour of the rights of others*

Authenticity and Humility	*Manipulation*
Self-existence is conditional upon the welfare of others	*Self-existence depends upon the approval of others*
Manipulates and uses own strength to benefit the general situation	*Manipulates and uses the weakness of others for personal benefit*

(d) Be Led By Your Reason

As mentioned earlier, all life forms are governed by survival instincts that operate intuitively and emotionally but our species is additionally equipped with an intellect that allows us to plan for longer and more durable means of ensuring survival. When this is overruled by emotional demands, we lose the essential quality that makes us human.

How often in a discussion have you heard the request, *"Be reasonable?"* The fundamentally important motive behind this simple request is that the person making it is becoming fearful at a subconscious level, that the other person is substituting an emotional response for a rational one.

We are defined by our capacity to think rationally. Not only do we have a capacity for knowledge that is vastly superior to our closest primal relatives, but we also have the ability to reason which allows us to use that knowledge wisely, *if we choose to do so.* If knowledge is powered only by emotion and not by the directive judgement of reason it will invariably result in chaos both in the lives of individuals and their societies. In the last century, for example, there was a growth of knowledge that was far greater than in any previous period. Politically, however, this was frequently supported by narrow tribally-based nationalism and not by reason, which resulted in slaughter, tribal genocide and state-sanctioned murder on a scale unprecedented in human history. Backed as it was by the technical resources of the modern world it became the darkest period in human history.

Emotions power actions and it is therefore imperative that we understand how and why these emotions are created so that we may control the process. In *all* life forms emotions arise as an instinctive response to outside stimuli but only in our species are those emotions potentially governed by a *self-directed* thinking process that can apply logic and reasoning. If we choose to use it, this vitally important ability allows us to develop greater and far more appropriate responses to outside stimuli.

If thoughts create emotions and emotions create actions, it is vital that the thoughts that start this process be correct interpretations of reality.

It has been suggested that individuals whose emotions are controlled by reason and logic function at an unfeeling level. The reverse, however, is true, in that individuals who are governed by reason are free from conflicting, out-of-control, and frequently inappropriate emotions. They are therefore *more* capable of directing their emotions towards more gratifying experiences which are genuine reflections of their growth and personal needs. Genuinely loving relationships, appreciation of the arts, dedication to an ideal or greater spiritual awareness, all of these are *more* accessible to the individual who can rationally direct their thoughts to achieving them. Individuals governed primarily by reason can allow themselves the luxury of dreams and creative imagination, knowing that it is their thoughts rather than instinct that create, sustain and guide them both. *Although we grow great by our dreams they must be controlled by the hand of logic and reason.*

Individuals whose emotions are not controlled by reason operate at the level of barbarism and will always be captives of conflicting and often mutually-destructive emotions that prevent them from operating at a more fulfilling level.

(e) Face Life With Fortitude

It is one of life's ironies that most individuals expect happiness as a right and the absence of it as a penalty. This is

understandable as in many ways we are biologically programmed to seek out happiness, pleasure and joy and to avoid
sadness, dissatisfaction and sorrow. This creates the illusion that
pain, suffering and grief are unjust rather than things just to be
avoided. This fantasy is at the heart of most human suffering and
is what prevents most people from facing life with strength and
fortitude.

Everything that exists does so through the balancing effect
of that which opposes it. Beauty, for example, cannot exist without ugliness, which therefore becomes a defining part of beauty.
Similarly justice, virtue, order, freedom and joy cannot exist
without injustice, vice, chaos, tyranny and sorrow. To expect
one without the other is futile, illogical and contrary to life. You
can certainly strive for one and do your best to avoid the other
and it is human nature to try to do so, but *you will not achieve
happiness without being prepared to experience sorrow.*

If it were possible to list and then eliminate everything in
life that caused you pain or sorrow, maintaining only that which
gave you pleasure, you would very quickly become unhappy
about things of less and less significance which is the psychological basis of neurosis.

The simple secret of facing life with fortitude is to fully and
unconditionally accept three facts that are unavoidable aspects
of your reality:

1) *If you want to experience joy, pleasure or happiness, you have
to be prepared to pay the price of pain. If you want to totally
avoid pain you will have to avoid all attempts at pleasure.*

2) *Everyone is born with significant limitations into a world
over which they have limited control. That world is neither
just nor unjust, good nor bad, fair nor unfair. These are
human concepts to which you may aspire, but they have no
basis in universal reality.*

3)   *Pain, sorrow and grief are not examples of cosmic injustice,
      a disordered universe or a vengeful God any more than
      happiness, joy and pleasure are examples of cosmic
      benevolence, universal order or a charitable deity. They are
      examples, not of chaos but of harmony and balance.*

When sadness strikes, as indeed it sometimes will, it often helps to "reason" it away. This cannot work immediately as the emotions intervene but their influence is less enduring when they are guided by reason.

> *A practical approach to lifting a sad mood is to write down a list of the things that currently make you sad and then on the same paper, a list of all the things that currently make you happy or for which you are grateful such as good friends, loving parents, health, living in a great country, fine mind, educational opportunities, etc. At the bottom of the page write, "I choose to be happy" and for the next week and several times daily remind yourself, "I choose to be happy because ---."*

Remember happiness and sadness are both *choices* that you make. We all have difficulties and unpleasant moments and many of these cannot be solved, as they are often simply a part of life. You *also* have blessings however, and you can choose to count these and be happy or to focus on your pain and be sad. This is something you *can* control.

You can choose to see "difficulties" as uninvited guests but your guests are *not you*. Observe them come, accept their visit and say goodbye as soon as possible and remember that the darkest moments in our lives are often like the darkest moments of the day. It is only then that we can really see the stars.

(f) Give Life a Chance and Take a Risk

As part of the foreword of this book I stated that life is a very special gift. In this context I am not merely referring to a happy or successful life, although of course this is an ideal. I am referring to the simple fact of being alive.

The various items of matter of which we are made have come together for a brief moment in time, as unique, sentient, animate and living beings capable of feeling, breathing, loving, appreciating, touching, seeing and Yes! of suffering, grieving and regretting. Each of us has our own opinion as to the source of this gift, but one thing is sure, many people do not use it to its full potential and many waste it. As with all gifts it should be assumed that it is given with the intention that it be used, cherished and enjoyed. How disappointed the giver of life must be to see how many are reluctant to do so.

It seems that in much of our western Judaeo/Christian tradition there is a strange history of life rejection built on a foundation of denial that suggests that there is something "sinful" in enjoying the pleasures of living. Indeed our *traditional* social culture often encourages the permanent delaying of life in favour of a possibly illusory future. This of course directly contradicts the more *contemporary* mandate of living for the moment. In later chapters I will discuss how these two apparently conflicting views can and should be reconciled.

It seems that for many people life is like an actor hovering in the wings of their own theatrical drama waiting patiently to make an entrance. When that entrance is fettered by unrealistic excuses, unreasonable demands and a need for escapism that masquerades as caution, life will never make its entrance and they will not have lived.

Look upon any crowded street at the number of people whose lives are vibrant with the joy of living and who embrace life and its often simple routines with a deep and enduring passion. What a joy these people are when you see them and how they enrich our lives. Unfortunately we do not see them often, instead we are more likely to see weary, dispirited-looking people whose lives are underwritten by a dull mediocrity and who creep around with no spark of animation in their eyes and no glorious purpose in their hearts. They are not living but merely playing a part while life waits patiently for the call that never comes. Although you cannot avoid remembering the glories of the past and equally should not avoid planning for tomorrow, you have to try to live in the present moment because ultimately that is the only place you can live. If all your time is spent remembering a past that has forever gone or in planning the dubious security of an unknown future, you are not living anywhere. As a Sanskrit poem from the Indian Vedantic tradition wisely describes it:

> *"Look well to this day, for it is life. It is the very life of life. It is that moment when the unforgiving past meets the unknown future and where these two great eternities have meaning. In the brief course of today lie all the verities and realities of your existence. The bliss of growth, the glory of action and the splendour of beauty. For yesterday is but a dream, and tomorrow is only a vision, but today well-lived makes every yesterday a dream of happiness and every tomorrow a vision of hope. Look well therefore to this day"*

What this is saying in contemporary terms is that the past, present and future are fluid components of your life and eternally flow through it. The past is the context which will guide tomorrow's mission and the present is your field of action. The question to be asked is: "What is your mission and how will today's actions achieve it?"

Try thinking about and applying some of the positive attitudes outlined below to your daily life and observe the difference they can make toward changing your perceptions of its daily challenges.

- *Your quality of life is determined by your own courage, determination and desire, not by your past or by external circumstances. These may strongly influence your life but they need not control your current actions.*

- *Much of your future is outside your immediate control and you cannot direct it. "What if" and "catastrophe" worrying about potential future events is a futile attempt to foresee and control the future. It is always wise to exercise reasonable caution, but excessive caution destroys the capacity to act. The wise individual who loves life generally knows the difference.*

- *Contrary to popular opinion, human beings are "process" directed, not goal-oriented. You need a goal to work towards, but the goal itself is secondary to the process of working towards it. Many people agonize so much over the suitability of the goal that this frequently replaces action by providing an excuse for non-action.*

- *Doing what you really want to do involves sacrifice. This is a valid consideration, but searching for negatives, however, should not be an excuse for non-action or non-acceptance of challenge.*

- *Learn to love. Unconditional love, freely given, is one of the main ways in which life can be expressed and through which the human spirit passes from selfishness to selfhood, from solitude to kinship, and from ignorance to understanding.*

- *Learn to endure your challenges with courage. Talent, wealth, influence, intellect and personal strength fade into insignificance before the power of endurance and personal courage. Remember, when a dying King Arthur was asked to whom he should leave his kingdom, he did not choose the wisest, strongest or most skilled among his knights, but replied simply but wisely, "I leave my kingdom to he who dares to take my sword."*

(g) Practise Self-love

In Chapter Six I will be looking at the vital importance of developing a viable, realistic and unconditionally loving self-image and the importance of this in the construction of a framework for effective living. In that chapter I will be using the process of "Vision Renaissance" to isolate and then deal with the various ways in which you limit your ability to truly love yourself. Let us look briefly, however, at the importance of genuine self-love.

Having a viable, realistic and unconditionally loving image of self is vitally important for two major reasons. Firstly it is only within the security of an unconditionally loving self-image that you can embrace the challenges, experiences and risks of life. The second is that you project your self-image by your words and actions and the outside world then acts upon them *as though they were true.* If you act as if you have value you will be valued for those qualities you proclaim. If you act as if you care and love who you are, that affection will be reciprocated. Conversely, if you act like a doormat you will be treated like one. The projected image, however, must not be an illusion; it must be honestly felt, sincerely constructed and authentic.

The basis of practising self-love is to be as gentle, non-judgemental and above all as understanding with yourself as you are to someone else you unconditionally love. The roots of self-development are just too tangled for you to be an effective judge of anyone, least of all yourself, and it is a psychological truism that self-judgement is often very harsh and cruel.

(h) Be Interested and Interesting

In the previous pages we have discussed the need to give life a chance. One of the most effective, immediate and practical ways you can do this is to be actively interested in the everyday world around you. Not only does this widen your personal knowledge and experience of the pleasure, variety and dynamism of life but it also dramatically extends your ability to connect with the people around you. Individuals who are interested in the world become interesting to others and attract them like a magnet. No individual who is *truly* interested and who is interesting as a result is ever lonely or bored.

Shakespeare tells us, *"Man in his time plays many parts."* This is true but Shakespeare was referring to those roles that are assumed automatically and not by choice: son, mother, parent, citizen, etc. These obviously have significant value, but to deeply widen your interest you have to strive actively for different activities that will provide you with many unique experiences.

In an effort to be "interesting", many people try to experience life vicariously through the lives of others, by books, films, radio and television. These forms of entertainment have merit and certainly widen the knowledge and scope of the individual, but at best they only give a second-hand understanding of the experience of others and are a poor substitute for the real thing. At worst, they can rapidly become an escape and an excuse for real experience.

As creatures of habit we often prefer to walk along a well-worn path which gives no challenge, rather than to seek a different path which although more arduous and less comfortable may lead to a more glorious view. *It is only by experience that you can experience* and there is no better way to enrich and ennoble your life, your emotions and your relationships, by exploring as many things as you can. Allow yourself to experience life and it will eventually lead you to the broader uplands of effective living.

How then do you become "interested" and "interesting"? The immediate answer is to be curious about life, meet and talk to as many people as possible, see as many places as you can, try as many things that interest you and which are within your grasp, find out how other people and cultures live, ask many, many questions and listen earnestly to the replies.

This book was written in Toronto, Canada, one of the most multicultural cities on earth. Within the mosaic of this vibrant city are scores of cultures, each with their own varieties of faith, food, music, literature, custom and tradition all waiting for the avid explorer. Forget for a moment the usual tourist haunts. Here is a list of the places in Toronto where you can broaden your horizons and see things you may never have seen before. A similar list can be constructed for any large city anywhere and at any time:

(a)   A service in an Islamic mosque
(b)   An Indian temple
(c)   A Buddhist temple
(d)   A Jewish synagogue
(e)   High mass at a cathedral
(f)   Coffee at a luxury hotel
(g)   The Royal Ontario Museum
(h)   A microbrewery
(i)   A session of parliament
(j)   A court hearing
(k)   A tour of City Hall
(l)   A spiritualist séance
(m)   A prison
(n)   A street market
(o)   A lesser-known art gallery
(p)   A guided tour of Roy Thomson Hall
(q)   A jazz club
(r)   A Greek wedding
(s)   A hostel for the homeless
(t)   One of dozens of ethnic restaurants
(u)   A hike along the Rosedale ravine
(v)   A radio broadcast station
(w)   A service at a spiritualist church
(x)   A monastery

(y)   A factory in full production
(z)   A behind-the-scenes theatre rehearsal

You will see that in the above list the alphabet has been exhausted but it only covers a fraction of the many things there are to see, do and experience in a big city. In addition, there are the regular theatre productions, arts festivals, concerts, special lecturing visitors and exhibitions that regularly come to any large city. This list, however, only covers the immediate locality. Widen this by just a three or four-hour car trip and you have a list that is virtually endless. Widen your geographic area still further and you can embrace foreign travel, where for a relatively modest outlay and a few financial sacrifices the world itself is at your feet. The catalogue of every library, municipal recreation office and community college is full of challenging, stimulating and interesting courses that are not just academic or business-related. The local adult education catalogue in front of me at this moment includes moderately-priced courses in Tibetan cooking, astrology, meditation, spirituality, winter hiking, alternative history and scores of others that can stimulate the mind, imagination and interest. The list is endless and the experience is everlasting.

(i) Dare to Dream and Dare to Act

Our species is uniquely blessed with the power and wonder of imagination. To a great degree it is our capacity to dream that powers an effective life and inspires great achievement. It is our imagination that created ancient monuments that inspire the human heart, musical masterpieces that fill us with passion, art and literature that continue to define our cultures, and imagination that stimulates science to probe relentlessly into unknown worlds. All are the products of imagination trying to contact the hidden forces that direct life itself. Individuals who dared to dream and who have implemented their dreams in the field of action realize, however, that it is not enough just to dream and to imagine. If imagination is not complemented by action it withers and dies or deteriorates into the lethargic indulgence of a daydream. The effective life distinguishes between daydreams and creative imagination and fuses creative imagination with determined action. Although the power of this combination is unbeatable, it is vitally important to understand both and how they complement each other. Let us look first at creative dreaming and then the type of action that is needed to bring it into reality.

Dreams, Daydreams and Creative Dreaming

The great advantage that we have over the animal kingdom is our ability to dream and to see beyond the bounds of ordinary vision. Although all life forms share a common world and have similar needs, human beings are unique in that we also have the power to transcend those needs by a deeper vision that can go beyond current reality and soar into new anticipated states of being. Even in the early days of our development it was obvious that this was a very special facility, because coupled with our ability to dream was the realization that our dreams were not merely fanciful pictures but were, in a sense, real and portrayed a state of being that was possible. It was realized by our forebears who faced a hostile and unforgiving world, that our unique weapon of survival was our capacity to dream creatively and to make those dreams real.

There are three types of dreams to consider. There are the subconscious reflections of our daily lives which come to us unbidden when we are sleeping. There are also daydreams which come to us when we are at rest and which are often temporary escapes from the duller aspects of our existence. These are harmless and helpful diversions that make life tolerable and should not be condemned, as in many ways they are no less a form of escape than art, music or literature. In their daydreams the poor become rich, the enslaved become free, the miserable find happiness and the lonely find the warmth, love and companionship they crave. Both these forms of dreaming have one element in common however, they come to us unbidden with no purposeful activity on our part.

The third type of dream however, is that which forms part of a framework for effective living. Creative dreaming is purposefully created and sustained by will, intense desire and an energy that manifests itself in the field of action. This is very close to that most unique of all human experiences – hope. Psychology cannot easily detect the stimulus for the difference between ordinary daydreams and creative imagination but the main difference is in result, because *intense and sustained desire becomes translated into its physical equivalent.*

This does not mean that every half-hearted daydream will materialize but it does mean that where desire is strong enough, where it is backed up with resolution and will, and where there is no conflict with natural law, desires and ideals are likely to be realized. It is this process that transforms a dreamer into a "doer."

The creative dreaming that leads to achievement has a distinctive pattern of growth that must be recognized and followed if the dream is to materialize. It starts with an understanding that we do not create our dreams any more than a computer creates its program. We are a channel through which a dream passes on its way to reality. However, this channel can only operate in an individual who has an open mind, who is flexible enough to see beyond obvious limitations and who can conceive other concepts, patterns and ways of doing things. To this individual, ideas emerge as if from nowhere and when they do, they take hold of them and inspire their imagination.

This feeling of inspiration then compels the successful dreamer to actively commit themselves to the fulfilment of their dream and in so doing they begin to see it as a reality rather than just a possibility. They then act upon that reality, adjusting their behaviour to accommodate every event that tries to divert them from their goal. This can be compared to that of an aircraft that flies from A to B. For most of its flight, it is off course because of the many variables associated with flying. Its destination, however, has been previously coded into its operating system and its flight path, speed and height are automatically adjusted to counteract these ongoing variables. It can be said that the aircraft has been committed to its destination. In individuals, this commitment involves a total and unflinching belief in the reality of the goal itself. The great American psychologist William James described this commitment well:

> *"The greatest revolution in our generation is the discovery that human beings, by changing the inner aspect of their mind, can change the outer aspect of their life. You only have to think in cold blood that the thing in question is real and it will become infallibly real and will become so knit with reason and emotion that it will be real. If you want to be rich you can be rich, if you want to be learned you can be learned, if you want to be happy you can be happy, but you must really wish for these things exclusively and not a hundred other things just as strongly."*

As an example, let us profile an individual who, as a real estate agent really wishes to become a leader in their field and whose desire for success is deeply felt. They see their success as a certainty and not a possibility, they dress as successful salesmen dress, drive what they drive and learn what they know so that they can also become experts at their craft. To achieve their goal they mix with those leaders of their profession who inspire rather than discourage, they see every rejection as a spur to greater effort and every expenditure of energy as a further step to their *inevitable* goal. In a world that has been slowed down to meet the needs of the slowest competitor an individual like this will generally succeed.

There comes a point, however, in the realistic development of every dream that the strength, courage and persistence of the dreamer is often tested by failure, challenge or defeat. It is almost as if this is needed in order for the dreamer to be worthy of their dream. It is here that many people fail, but if they persist, if they accept their defeats, if they can carry on bruised yet undaunted, it is likely that victory will eventually be theirs.

It is at this point that dreams often become energized by the self-sacrificing commitment of the dreamer and take off on their own, expanding in directions that could not have been envisaged by the dreamer. The dream of two young Americans of building a 50-pound bi-plane glider in North Carolina in 1900 became a 3000-ton rocket travelling to the far reaches of our solar system; the dream of two young American doctors to start a progressive modern medical facility became the Mayo clinic, one of the finest medical facilities in the world; and Marconi's dream of creating a wireless telegraphy system became a global information network that has revolutionized our system of communication.

Appropriate Action

It is not enough, however, just to dream and to imagine. If these are not complemented by action they rapidly fade away or become self-indulgent escapes from reality. Individuals who live effectively know the difference between daydreams and creative imagination and power the latter with determined and appropriate action. What do we mean by determined and appropriate action? The action that is needed to bring a dream into reality is a developmental one that starts with *planning* and progresses through to *implementation* and finally to the *perseverance* needed to bring it to completion. Let us look first of all at planning.

Many people are inclined to believe that creative dreaming and thinking about their dream is part of the planning process. Although it is certainly essential, it is not planning. Planning involves the *active* structuring of a strategic plan of action. It means comprehensive research, networking, the recording of every developmental aspect of the plan, time frames, activities within those time frames, interim goals and criteria for evaluating progress. Effective plans of action have to be self-adjusting, which means that built within them is the ability to recognize and deal with unforeseen events that tend to lead away from the goal. The more comprehensive a plan is in this area, the greater the likelihood that the goal will be achieved. Effective planning is not a passive activity but an intensely active one that reinforces the initial commitment that is essential to the achievement of a goal.

Effective planning, however, is only part of the action that is needed. Many people plan, some more effectively than others, but for many that is where it ends because their plans never move into the implementation stage. The originators never take the plunge and convert their plans into action. They remain on the beach wistfully gazing at the water and as an excuse for their lack of action concentrate further on perfecting their plan. There comes a time, and this should also be part of an effective planning process, when planning has to be replaced by forceful and determined action. There will be mistakes, unforeseen events and frustrations many of which should have been anticipated in the planning process, but these are part of the process of implementation. I'm reminded of the overly cautious mother who insisted that her child not go into the pool until they had learned to swim, implying, of course, that swimming is a skill that can be learned on land. You can certainly learn about swimming theory and safety techniques without entering the water and you should do so, but there comes a time when you have to jump in and hope that the theory will work in practice.

The third part of the process of determined action is *perseverance.* When we act to achieve a dream our resources will be tested. It is here that the advantages of dedicated commitment are most obvious. Achieving a dream is often like a long and tough race. In the early stage there are many competitors and the odds of winning are quite remote but after a while when fatigue sets in, some competitors drop out and the odds are reduced. Later still, when the going gets much tougher, more drop out and the chances of winning begin to increase dramatically until only a few competitors remain. It is here, however, that life often differs, in that the proceeds of victory are so abundant that the final winners all share them. As Samuel Johnson wisely pointed out, *"Great works are performed not by strength but by perseverance."* Perseverance is not an avoidance of action but the spiritual equivalent of it, and the gentle courage that it demands is usually invincible.

Victory will always go to the individual who pursues their goal with courage, but there are two types of courage. There is the courage of determined and forceful action and the courage of passive and committed endurance. The effective individual recognizes and practises both and in combining this with the magic of a creative imagination becomes unbeatable. A Sanskrit proverb describes this combination well:

"When you are the anvil, bear; when you are the hammer, strike."

SUMMARY OF CHAPTER TWO

The main identifying traits presented by an individual who lives effectively are:

- *A trust in their own personal judgement*

- *A patient and a mature respect for the value and significance of time*

- *A sincere humility and respect for the identity and values of others*

- *A primary reliance upon reasoned judgement*

- *Fortitude in the face of difficulty*

- *The ability to take a chance and to "embrace" life*

- *A practised self-love*

- *The desire to be both interested and interesting*

- *An ability to dream creatively and to act with determination*

Chapter Three

SELF-UNDERSTANDING

"Not in the clamour of a crowded street, not in the shouts and plaudits of the throng, but in ourselves are triumph and defeat."   Henry W. Longfellow

"Every man's enemy is within himself."   Bahya

"The first principle of self-understanding is that you must not fool yourself, because you are the easiest person to fool."   Richard Feynman

"Everyone thinks of changing the world, but no one thinks of changing himself."   Leo Tolstoy

"You improve yourself by victories over yourself. There must be contests and you must win."   Edward Gibbon

"Everyone is just about as happy as they decide they are going to be."   Abraham Lincoln

"Generally children do not think; they interpret and imitate."   Anonymous

"Your mental attitude is something you can control outright and you must use self-discipline until you create a Positive Mental Attitude -- your mental attitude attracts to you everything that makes you what you are."   Napoleon Hill

"The last of the human freedoms is to choose one's attitude in any given set of circumstances and to choose one's own way."   Dr. Viktor E. Frankl

"You cannot control what happens to you, but you can control your attitude toward what happens to you, and in that, you will be mastering change rather than allowing it to master you."   Brian Tracy

As indicated above, your life is governed by the way you inter-pret events and not by the events themselves. In "Vision Renais-sance", I call this collection of statements that shapes your life, your "Vision."

THE DEVELOPMENT OF YOUR PERSONAL VISION

Let us now look at how and why a personal vision is created and developed. It is *imperative* that this process be understood before looking at your own personal Vision and beginning to isolate those areas of it that may hinder you from an effective life.

As individuals you are born into a *potentially* hostile world about which nothing is known but you are born with *biologi-cal imperatives* and *inherited tendencies* that ensure survival. A biological imperative is a natural and instinctive survival mech-anism that compels you to act in a certain way. In human beings and in their early formative years these two major imperatives are *fear* and *conformity*.

Faced with any *new* experience, fear makes you withdraw as much as possible, both mentally and physically, to a position of security in order to gain information about the new experience. Conformity compels you to try to be the same as the environ-ment around you in order to hide from danger. Although these two factors, namely *fear* and the need to *conform,* assist in your survival, they are paradoxically the same factors that can in later years limit and often prevent your growth into the fullness of life. *Your biological instinct is oriented only to your survival and procreation and not to your spiritual or personal growth.*

Having retreated to a position of comfort and security when faced with a new experience, you look for information from your environment that will guide you in dealing with it. Remember for the moment that we are only talking about *new* experiences. In a newborn baby, and to a gradually lessening extent a growing child, most experiences are new, and *all* have to be evaluated in this manner.

Having received as much information as possible, usually from parents, family and friends, a conscious survival decision is made about how to act regarding the new experience. In future, I will refer to this experience as being the *"stimulating agent."* A stimulating agent is anything (person, place, event, sound or experience) that produces a response.

These survival decisions are made in a very specific way by answering an internally felt question that is structured as follows:

"Faced with this new event, and based upon the information that I have received about it, what must I do, and what will be the negative consequences if I do not?"

It is vitally important for you to understand that it is this question, and the various ways you answer it, which forms the core of your vision and the basis of Vision Renaissance for they will create both your actions and the emotions which will power them. *The answers, however, may be wrong, irrational or inappropriate to your growth and therefore creative of inappropriate emotions and behaviour.*

Having now acted in accordance with data previously received, the baby (child, growing adult) watches the resulting feedback. *Did my actions help me? Do I feel better? Am I more (or less) secure?* This feedback becomes additional data and either strengthens, weakens or replaces the original belief. If it becomes apparent over time that the resultant feedback is life-enhancing and generally appropriate to your immediate survival, the statement (attitude) that has evaluated that part of your reality becomes part of your subconscious and automatic operating system *even though it may have been based on an incorrect or inappropriate interpretation of that reality.*

From this moment your reasoning process, which initially justified your actions, is bypassed and similar events are automatically *"claimed"* by the belief that previously evaluated it. This will create emotions and actions that are *appropriate to the belief* but not necessarily to your well-being. In future I will refer to this belief statement as an "Attitude." The following diagram (Fig. 1) shows how this process develops from stimulating agent to affirming (or negating) feedback.

DIAGRAM OF PERSONAL GROWTH
FIGURE 1

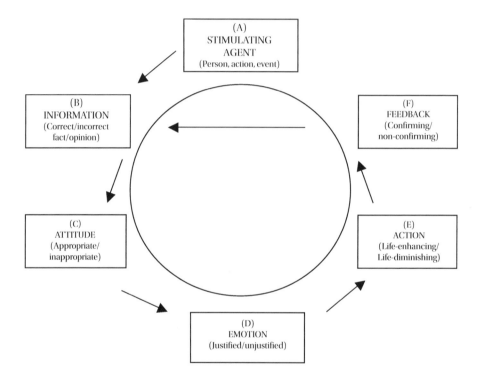

A = <u>Stimulating agent</u>. *Any action, event, place or thing that creates an emotional response.*

B = <u>Collection of information</u>. *Usually from parents, family or friends. The main consideration here is whether this information was correct/incorrect or opinion/factually based.*

C = <u>Attitude</u>. *Based on the information received in (B) about (A),* "What must I do in this situation and what do I think will happen if I do not?" *Is the statement a logical and accurate reflection of the situation and (bearing in mind that this creates your emotions and actions), is it appropriate to your well-being, survival and goals?*

D = <u>Emotion</u>. The attitude in (C) determines the type of emotion (D) needed to act (fear, envy, anger, joy, anticipation, etc). *Is the emotion created here justified?*

E = <u>Action</u>. The action taken in (E) and the emotion needed for it (D) are both created by the attitude in (C) *not* by the event (A). *Will this action help or hinder your survival, well-being or the attainment of your goals?*

F = <u>Feedback</u>. The feedback that confirms and strengthens, or denies and weakens, the validity of the attitude. This then becomes part of the information base of (B).

There are three *vital* aspects of this process, which are central to the philosophy of Vision Renaissance.

It is not the stimulating event that creates an emotion and its subsequent action, but the pre-programmed attitude that previously interpreted similar events.

If the attitude that resulted from the previous interpretation was incorrect, or if originally correct, not adjusted to changing circumstances, it will produce emotions and subsequent actions that may be inappropriate, irrational or destructive.

Attitudes that do not lead to an effective and fulfilling life can be isolated and changed from life-diminishing ones to ones that are life-enhancing.

It will be obvious from the above that the emotions that power actions are not usually caused by the initial event but are stimulated by pre-programmed attitudes which previously evaluated similar events. In other words, the way you see life, the way you interpret the realities of life and the statements that you make in your head about life, shape your entire existence. They govern your emotions, colour your personality, control your relationships with other people and even ultimately determine the health of your body. In other words, health and happiness begin in the head, not in the things that happen to you, but in the way you see those things and interpret them, not as they are but as you are.

A simple example will demonstrate this important point. You are standing at a bus stop one cold winter morning, when someone behind you aggressively bumps into you without apologizing. You turn angrily, ready to give this rude person a "piece of your mind", when at the last moment you notice that he has a white stick and is blind. What happens to the angry emotion? It disappears, and is probably replaced by pity and maybe guilt. *The initiating event* is of course the same, but the attitude which powered your actions has changed from: "I'd better get ready to protect myself from this man *OR ELSE* I may be in danger" to "I must help this weaker person *OR ELSE* I will feel ashamed."

You have "attitudes" which evaluate every aspect of your reality. These increase every time a new event occurs and having gathered sufficient information, you decide on an appropriate response. You have, for example, "attitudes" about aging, youth, dying, wealth, success, social obligation, other people, marriage, divorce and for all other aspects of your personal life.

Although many of your attitudes are appropriate to your well-being, there are often many others that can dramatically hinder your growth into the fullness of life.

Exercise #1

It is important to note that an attitude is generally a felt statement of what you should do when faced with a certain circumstance followed generally by an "OR ELSE" statement which describes the negative consequences that may likely follow if you do not.

The following exercise will *begin* the process of focusing on the type of life-diminishing statements that *many* people regularly live by. *All of them are toxic, irrational and life-limiting.*

When you have *more* than a few moments, please think objectively and with an open mind about two or three areas of your life that are not completely fulfilling. Those areas could include, but certainly not be limited to, your relationships, job, use of time, lack of excitement, attitude to criticism, ability to love, procrastination, status, decision-making ability, ability to "let your hair down," excessive caution, lack of self-confidence, etc. Take your time to do this. When you have done so, write them down and *carefully* review each of the following statements noting whether any apply to you and the identified situation.

LIST OF COMMON ERRORS IN OUR BELIEF SYSTEM

(1) I should keep my feelings to myself *OR ELSE* I may hurt other people's feelings and they won't like me.

(2) I must be successful, competent or talented in at least one area of my life *OR ELSE* I will be a failure and will have no value.

(3) I have to please others and satisfy their expectations *OR ELSE* I will be a failure.

(4) I must be loved (approved) by all those who are significant in my life *OR ELSE* I cannot love and approve myself.

(5) I should take on the problems of other people *OR ELSE* I will see myself as an uncaring person.

(6) I must put other people's needs before mine *OR ELSE* I will be seen (see myself) as self-centred and uncaring.

(7) I cannot admit and proclaim my talents; *IF I DO* people will see me as conceited.

(8) I must always be busy with some profitable or worthwhile endeavour *OR ELSE* I will be wasting valuable time.

(9) People have to be watched all the time *OR ELSE* they will take advantage of, use or manipulate me.

(10) People are generally not grateful for what I do for them *AND THEREFORE* I don't bother with them.

(11) Most people are basically selfish and only care about their own feelings *AND THEREFORE* I am not going to waste my time reaching out to them.

(12) My life is completely determined by outer circumstances *AND THEREFORE* I cannot be bothered to try and change it.

(13) My life could end tomorrow *AND THEREFORE* I will direct all my efforts to the present moment.

(14) Life must work out just the way I planned *OR ELSE* it will be terrible and I will be unhappy.

(15) I had better take for myself everything that is immediately available *OR ELSE* everyone else will.

(16) Life is full of obstacles and problems *THEREFORE* I will not seek out new experiences.

(17) I must be loved (approved) by all those who are significant to me *OR ELSE* I will have no value.

(18) I must know in advance that other people love me and approve of me before I reach out to them *OR ELSE* they will use me for their own purposes.

(19) I must be in control of most situations or avoid them completely *OR ELSE* I will be in danger.

(20) I cannot easily forgive others *BECAUSE* if I do, I will see myself as losing and they will see me as weak. I will then be vulnerable and in danger and this will weaken my self-esteem.

Now, having selected one or more of the above statements that you feel *may* influence the identified areas:

(a)   briefly describe that situation in the space below.

(b)   indicate at least one major reason why you think the statement is not logical.

(c)   finally, and without writing anything down, ask yourself: "Why do I believe in the statement if it is not logical?" A couple of examples follow.

I often believe in the following attitude statements that influence the situation in my life described below and I make many of my decisions in accordance with this belief.

First Example

Statement:
I must be loved (approved) by all those who are significant to me OR ELSE I will have no value (statement #17 above).

Life situation:
Socially, I often try to guess what others like in people and then try to act like that. This is exhausting. When they don't approve of me I feel that I have no value and then get upset or depressed.

The above attitude statement is illogical because:

1) The significant people in my life all have *different* values and needs and it is impossible to be all things to all people. If I make my value dependent upon factors outside my control I am sabotaging my ability to grow. I cannot be approved by *everyone.*

2) If my value depends upon the love/approval of others, I must be lovable/approvable *all* the time. This is impossible.

3) Even if I wanted to change, to meet the approval of others, certain things *cannot* be changed i.e. my gender, physical appearance, race, culture and intellect. I am again measuring my own *internal* sense of value by something *outside* of my control.

4) If I *could* gain the approval of others *all* the time, it would take up so much time to get it that I could not pursue anything else. This, in itself, would defeat most of my personal goals.

5) If I did get the approval of most people but failed to get it from just one significant person, I would still have no value *by my definition.*

6) There may be people who are significant to me, whose approval I crave, who, *for their own reasons*, are not able to love or approve of anyone.

Second Example

Statement:
I must be successful, competent or talented in at least one area of my life OR ELSE I will be a failure and will have no value. (Statement # 2)

Life situation:
I often see many people who are more successful than I am, and when I do, it often makes me feel frustrated and a failure.

The above attitude statement is illogical because:

1) There are billions of people and only thousands of "competencies." Statistically, if for no other reason, it is *impossible* for *everyone* to be highly competent at *something*.

2) My culture may have defined "success" and "failure" but I have not. Nor have I thought about the sacrifices and "failures" needed to achieve it or whether I would make them. Until I do this, it is irrational for me to judge *either* failure *or* success.

3) If my life is valued quantitatively in terms of success, then I have to measure how much success qualifies. This is impossible, as success is qualitative and subjective.

4) If success could be measured by quality or quantity, what relationship would that have to my value? If this cannot be defined why base my value upon it?

5) If success *can* be measured, where do the millions who fall below me on that scale fit in? Am I in the top percentile? Am I by comparison more successful and therefore more valuable? And how can this be measured? If it does not make sense to put my value above others why would it make sense to put my value below theirs?

Exercise # 1 Continued

Now, using these two examples and the list of common errors above (1 – 20) as a guide, select at least two attitude statements that in your opinion control, direct or influence those areas of your life that you have indicated are limited in some way.

First Example

Attitude Statement:

_____

_____

Life situation: (Describe a situation that may be affected by the above)

_____

_____

_____

The above attitude statement is illogical because:

_____

_____

_____

_____

_____

Questions for personal reflection:

If the above statement is illogical (unreasonable) – why do you act as though it were true?

_____

_____

_____

If the actions the above statement creates are not appropriate to your feelings of well-being, do not help you achieve your goals or hinder your life in any way, why do you do them and where do you think that the belief that causes them may have come from? *(See if you can isolate the developmental or environmental input that created this belief – childhood, parental messages, social/religious/political background)*

<u>Second Example</u>

Attitude Statement:

_____

_____

_____

Life situation: (Describe a situation that may be affected by the above)

_____

_____

_____

The above attitude statement is illogical because:

_____

_____

_____

_____

_____

Questions for personal reflection:

If the above statement is illogical (unreasonable) – why do you act as though it were true?

_____

_____

_____

If the actions the above statement creates are not appropriate to your feelings of well-being, do not help you achieve your goals or hinder your life in any way, why do you do them and where do you think that the belief that causes them may have come from? *(See if you can isolate the developmental or environmental input that created this belief — childhood, parental messages, social/religious/political background)*

_____

_____

_____

_____

WHY YOU ACT UPON INAPPROPRIATE BELIEFS

A reasonable question that can now be asked is: "Why do I develop and then act upon an inappropriate belief if it does not help me?" The inappropriate attitudes that you have developed are formed in either of two distinct ways. Either they were based on a *correct* and *appropriate* interpretation of reality at the time, but with changing circumstances are no longer applicable or appropriate, or they were based on an *incorrect interpretation* of reality at the time and remain that way. Let us look at a couple of examples of both.

An individual is born into a small family consisting of a mother, father and a couple of siblings. In the process of establishing their value and significance within that unit, the individual quite correctly determines that their worth is strongly demonstrated by and is dependent upon the expressed approval of the family. This is obviously a *correct* and life-enhancing interpretation of reality, because if the individual was not approved, they would suffer the severe consequences of emotional neglect. The family's acceptance forms the basis of a harmonious family structure. In this instance the individual would probably adopt a belief that *correctly* suggests:

"I must be approved by all those who are significant to me OR ELSE I will not be accepted, will have no value and will be unhappy."

The difficulty occurs, of course, when years later the individual's spectrum of significant people has widened from the original four to a significantly greater number. If they are not consciously aware of this developing change, or if no specific incident has forced them to do so, they will still be seeking the approval of the scores of significant people with whom they come in daily contact. These would obviously include friends, business associates, employers, co-workers, extended family members and many others whose *universal* and *regular* approval could not be obtained. It would only be this however, that, by their definition would give them acceptance, approval and value. Their original belief is now no longer appropriate because their circumstances have changed.

As a second example let us look at the Attitude that might be adopted by an individual raised in a dogmatically religious household. In this instance, belief in a vengeful and tyrannical God might prevail: an all-powerful God whose affection can only be obtained by following rigid rules of behaviour. In such a family an individual who did not obey the rules would be seen as an outcast, loved neither by God, the family nor, by extension, the community. An *appropriate* attitude may then be developed which would suggest that:

"As God loves me conditionally, I'd better meet his conditions OR ELSE he and those around me will not love me."

Unless in later life the individual becomes aware of the inaccuracy of this statement, they will probably be plagued by unwarranted guilt, emotional tyranny and internal rejection, especially if their initial vision of God was one of an all-powerful tyrant.

The two beliefs referred to above arise from *correct and appropriate interpretations* of reality, which at a later date are no longer valid. Let us now look at those life-diminishing ones, which arise from an *incorrect* and *faulty* interpretation.

A child, wanting attention, eagerly rushes up to a well-loved and loving father when he comes in from work late at night. The father, a hard worker who works long hours and is justifiably tired, gently rebuffs the child, *"Be quiet dear and play with your toys."* He may be supported by his wife in the process, possibly getting mildly irritable if the child persists. A child generally interprets events emotionally rather than logically, and so if the rejection is repeated often enough and over a long enough period it may well be interpreted as:

> *"I am not important and my needs have no value, THEREFORE I will avoid asserting them in any way."*

Again, if this statement is acted upon later in life, and not challenged either by awareness or dramatically changed circumstances, the individual will find it difficult to assert their needs, preferences or desires. This will prevent the development of an authentic and happy life.

When stored Attitudes are stimulated, they create emotions and actions that can be detrimental. These beliefs are usually only challenged and changed when events are so new or traumatic that there is insufficient data for them to be evaluated. The underlying Attitudes then have to then be consciously reassessed. Individuals who are suddenly fired from a job may be compelled to reassess their attitudes towards criticism; a wife fleeing with children and limited resources from an abusive marriage may be obliged to re-evaluate her attitude to her own resources, self-esteem and self-sufficiency; and an individual faced with a terminal illness may review their attitude to life. It is these moments of genuine trauma that often reveal an individual's finest resources and in a moment of personal revelation they often see that part of their life has been lived under the influence of an illusion. Let us look at this entire process in the following true-life situation.

A student in one of my "Effective Living" courses provided an excellent practical example of a life lived under the influence of a toxic attitude which was dramatically changed by an "ah-ha" moment of personal awareness. I will call the young lady "Suzie." Suzie was attractive and well educated, with a good job and a delightful personality. One evening after several seminars Suzie stayed behind to discuss an unsatisfactory area of her life, namely the limited duration of her romantic relationships. Suzie wanted to get married and although she had no problem finding potential partners, her relationships abruptly ended when the question of marriage was raised. Suzie did not know why this was and wanted to discuss it. The "Effective Living" seminars which are part of the "Renewal Networks" personal growth groups, use talks, meditation, group dynamics, personal discussion and self-evaluated questionnaires to develop a dynamic framework for self-understanding and growth. During the course of these discussions Suzie's story emerged, and it will help us to understand how one's beliefs can be changed by a moment of awareness.

Suzie is the daughter of an engineer, an intelligent, practical but apparently somewhat impatient man, and the sister of two older brothers whose interests leaned to those of the father. In the early stage of Suzie's development, she tries to conform by participating in the family discussions that were generally limited to "guy-related" issues. In this particular family (*though fortunately not in all*) she is belittled by her brothers, as little sisters sometimes are, *"You're a girl – says one brother, what do you know about it?"* and clearly patronized by her father. Still needing to be accepted, but noting that conformity isn't working, she receives much needed attention by behaving badly. This, of course, fails, as she is then regularly reprimanded. Still needing to be "accepted", she carefully observes her environment.

One hot summer evening Suzie asks her father if he would like a cold beer. She gets him one and is rewarded with a smile and words of appreciation. Whilst this in itself is not sufficient to generate a survival attitude, it does contribute to the formation of one. Later Suzie volunteers to search for and eventually finds one brother's lost schoolwork and helps the other with his home study, each time being approved and appreciated. *"Hey, Suzie's changing – she's not a brat anymore"*, one brother comments, and her father notes with relief that *"Suzie's growing up at last."* Suzie has found her survival belief. We all need to be wanted and loved and Suzie now realizes that if she wants to be lovable she has to be useful. This *interpretation* of her personal reality is recorded by her subconscious mind as:

"I must be useful OR ELSE I will not be lovable."

For Suzie the statement is perfect because she thinks it gives her all that she needs. The problem is that it is an *incorrect* interpretation of reality. It is to be assumed that her family loved her, irrespective of her usefulness and just as she is, *but this was not apparent.* Twenty-five years later she is an attractive, clever and successful young woman who can be loved for her many other assets, but she continues to see herself as lovable only if she is useful. Suzie is therefore never short of suitors, as many people have built-in antennas that can detect useful people from afar. Suzie is the one going to watch the baseball match with her boyfriend on a wet Saturday afternoon instead of shopping with her girlfriends and is the one who stays up late typing her boyfriend's business reports or helping him paint his new apartment. Why? Because she wants to be loved and she *"knows"* that to be loved she has to be useful.

Suzie's dramatic moment of awareness always came when marriage was proposed. This new aspect of reality had to be evaluated rationally and consciously, thereby overriding her previous attitude to relationships. It was then that she realized that her proposed partners were motivated more by her usefulness to them rather than their love for her, and it was this harsh reality that invariably challenged the relationship.

In the process of *"Vision Renaissance"* it will be seen that the identification of a life-diminishing attitude is much harder than its elimination and replacement. Suzie's "ah-ah" moment came when she understood not only that her current relationships were based upon her belief that she had to be useful, but that her initial relationships created the belief in the first place. This changed her outlook dramatically and freed her of the need to be useful as a condition of being loved.

Several months later Suzie partnered with an individual who loved her for her very many lovable attributes, and they were married shortly thereafter.

Change and healing can only be achieved, however, when a life-diminishing attitude has been so clearly identified *that there is no doubt as to its authenticity.*

WHY OUR BELIEFS ARE INITIALLY DEVELOPED

"Guiding" beliefs are initially developed for reasons of psychological economy in that they allow us the opportunity to face new events and determine our reaction to them. All life forms have a biological tendency to wholeness, and nowhere is this developmental urge more defined than in the way data from new experience is accumulated, recorded and used.

This "tendency to wholeness" requires you to keep learning, as that is how your security is enhanced. You could not do this if *every* time you experienced an event you had to learn about it again and then re-evaluate it in order to determine a reaction. If you did so even simple acts like getting out of bed would be exercises in continuing observation, caution and decision-making. You would listen for sounds of danger before opening your eyes and realizing that it was safe would then carefully look around, making sure that the room was safe to proceed. You would then rise cautiously, making sure that nothing dangerous was under the bed, and would finally enter the bathroom with equal care, making sure once again that no one was lying in wait.

Although this is an exaggerated scenario, it is important to realize that you do *not* do this because you know from previous experience that in *your* bedroom, in *your* environment and *at this time,* you are perfectly safe. These assumptions, however, are only developed from prior experience and evaluation. This process categorizes and stores perceptions, judgements and conclusions for later use in order to move on to ever-widening observations, experience and growth.

FACTORS INFLUENCING THE PROCESS OF CHANGE

In all living things and especially with human beings there are two major forces that appear to conflict. These operate at both the biological and psychological levels and strongly influence our need for change and our capacity to effect it. This apparent conflict is between our survival needs as living organisms and the growing demands of our developing individuality and selfhood. In lower life forms this distinction is almost non-existent but in mankind it is far more pronounced and the sense of discord more acute. This arena of conflict has been somewhat dramatically described as the battleground upon which the integrating forces of spirit and the disintegrating forces of matter meet.

The conflict, however, is apparent rather than real, in that the urge to fulfil the growing demands of our own individuality is an extension of and grows out of our more basic survival instincts. The sense of conflict however, is very real.

In the following pages I will describe how these two conflicting forces both resist and encourage change.

FORCES WHICH RESIST CHANGE

It is important to realize that the biological forces that direct our survival will resist all attempts at change and will, where appropriate, sabotage our efforts to do so. The biological imperative of nature *in its early stages* is physical survival and *not* growth. The urge for personal fulfilment and the enhancing of personal understanding through self-gratifying experiences grow out of this but operate at a psychological rather than biological level. Change represents risk and risk is contrary to physical survival. The message received, and then usually acted upon by individuals is,*"You may be unfulfilled, overindulgent or bored but whatever you are doing you have survived up to this point, so you must be doing something right – don't rock the boat."* This is the undermining influence that occurs whenever an individual tries to shed a bad habit. A person starting a new diet, for example, will regularly check their weight *every morning,* perhaps even knowing that generally in the first few days little weight is lost and some is gained. After just two or three days of nominal weight loss, they stop the diet and retreat from the process (risk) of change; an individual quits smoking or excessive drinking and seeks out social activities that encourage both; another decides to spend more time with their family and less time working, but without consciously realizing it, seeks out a new project; a young woman fleeing from a controlling and limiting relationship looks for similar men, preferring an anguished security over the fear and risk of change; and a person seeking ways of defeating a lack of decision-making ability may create new and more complex decision-making scenarios.

In these examples, individuals do not actively seek out self-defeating behaviours but rather are unaware of the internal forces compelling them *not* to change. The difficulty, of course, is that although basic survival needs resist change, your psychological need for growth demands it and often with an ever-increasing sense of urgency. At any point in time you are either progressing to a fuller life or retreating from it. This is because your physical needs favour non-action and your psychological ones favour progressive movement and growth.

One way in which a resistance to growth and change is apparent is the way people rationalize their limiting beliefs. Self-limiting attitudes are like parasites in one's mind. They escape exposure by hiding behind or feeding upon other more rational beliefs. Even when you have identified a limiting attitude there is a tendency to try to rationalize it rather than face its reality. Let us for example refer back to the previous example of "Suzie." Suzie measured her ability to be loved as being directly dependent upon her capacity to be useful by believing "*I must be useful OR ELSE I will not be lovable.*" Having isolated this, the tendency in many people (though fortunately not in Suzie) would then be to try to rationalize it. *"What's wrong with being useful?" "I like to be useful, it makes me feel good,"* or *"Everyone loves because they need and can use people, so what's wrong with what I think?"* What is "wrong" is that they ignore Suzie's basic toxic premise: "*I am ONLY lovable if I am useful.*"

Another area of self-deception is the substitution of words that appear to be similar but which are not. This is another form of self-sabotage. For example "I must be kind or I will not be lovable, and what's wrong with being kind?" This is generally a *true* statement as unkind people are not very lovable, but kindness and usefulness are NOT the same. Usefulness is often a form of manipulation; kindness usually arises from genuine compassion.

In the Vision Renaissance programme, which starts in the next chapter, the spotlight of honest and relentless understanding is brought to the specific and accurate isolation of limiting beliefs.

INFLUENCES THAT ENCOURAGE CHANGE

Although our biological make-up tends to resist change, there is a competing psychological imperative that challenges inaction and directs it to growth, wider experience and wholeness. This is both the cause of hope and of conflict. If followed, it leads to integration and a fuller life; if resisted, it will lead to decay and disintegration. This tendency to wholeness is especially pronounced in the human species where it operates at both the biological and psychological levels. It is this which encourages change, especially when a limiting attitude is *clearly recognized* by an epiphany moment that says *"This is it."* This urge to growth and experience strongly challenges the influences that discourage a person's development. The dynamics of this *tendency to wholeness* have eluded science, as they appear to operate in a non-physical manner. Within each living cell there appears to exist the genetic programme of the complete and fully-formed organism to which all development is directed. Even though each cell is *functionally* different at any one time, this design, to which every activity of the organism is directed, is inherent in all of them.

It is this tendency to wholeness and completion that integrates, organizes and directs every activity of an organism towards its goal. This directive capacity, though internally felt, often seems to be externally driven. Attempts to explain the origin of this have ranged from the great American botanist Edmund Sinnott's belief that *all* human activity is derived from a physical (though not yet identified) source, through to the spiritual constructs which suggest that such processes are God-directed and inspired.

Edmund Sinnott, in defending his theory of purely physical cause admitted, however, that although he could see a clear physical connection governing all steps of biological development, he was baffled as to how the process itself was maintained, *" ...but how a plant or a small mass of embryonic cells, has all its parts so closely coordinated at every step of evolution that an organic self-adjusting system is produced and maintained is still beyond our comprehension."*

In all living things this growth pattern is identified in three ways. *First*, it proceeds in a regular, clearly-defined and *predictable* manner toward a pre-determined goal *as though* being specifically directed. *Second*, that within the genes of a species there is a definite form and quality common to all its members and to which individual growth tends to conform, and *third*, if normal development is disturbed, a series of processes tend to restore it. Injuries are healed, missing parts are frequently regenerated and altered patterns of growth are initiated so that a whole and typical individual tends to be produced.

There is a clear indication here that all organisms *"want"* to be physically whole and that when growth and development are disturbed, they will actively seek and support life-enhancing alternatives. In the human species this imperative is additionally and strongly felt at the psychological level. This principle of growth, was reaffirmed by the eminent zoologist E. Russell, who wrote, *"If, in a living animal, normal structure and functional relations, either external or internal, are disturbed, activities will usually be set in train that are directive towards restoring structural and functioning norms, or establishing new norms which are adapted to altered circumstances."*

In contemporary terms this means that our *natural* inclination is to progress into ever-expanding arenas of experience and challenge and if this is interrupted, physical and psychological processes are usually set in motion to overcome it. These are expressed psychologically by dissatisfaction, moments of insight which inspire change, and the "flatness" we often feel when we have finally achieved a longed for goal and are then stimulated to find another.

SUMMARY OF CHAPTER THREE

1. For reasons of psychological economy and to encourage growth we develop and retain beliefs that evaluate and then determine responses to life situations.

2. It is these pre-programmed beliefs that direct emotional responses and subsequent actions and not the stimulating events themselves.

3. These beliefs, which we refer to as "Attitudes" may be toxic, life-limiting and incorrect interpretations of current reality.

4. Incorrect "Attitudes" are developed either as *correct* interpretations of a previous reality but which are not currently realistic or as *incorrect* interpretations of reality when they were constructed.

5. "Attitudes" are structured as mentally formed statements, which direct behaviour and which warn of the consequences of not following that direction.

6. Survival instincts resist change and the identification of life-diminishing beliefs. However, this resistance is challenged to a significant degree by the tendency to wholeness, which is physically inherent in all living things. This tendency is most strongly represented at both the physical and psychological levels in the human species.

7. This conflict is generally overcome once a life-diminishing belief has been so correctly identified that there is no doubt as to its authenticity.

Chapter Four

CONTACTING YOUR BELIEF SYSTEM

"True wisdom lies in knowing the cause of things."
                                            Anonymous Greek philosopher

"Self-knowledge is the beginning of wisdom."   *Attributed to Socrates*

"The doorstep to the temple of wisdom is the knowledge of our own ignorance."
                                            Charles Haddon Spurgeon

" Men who know themselves are no longer fools; they stand on the threshold of the Door of Wisdom."
                                            Havelock Ellis

A Greek philosopher once described true wisdom as *"knowing the cause of things."* One might be tempted to add *"and the courage to search for those causes."* Indeed if you are to change those parts of your belief system that hinder you from living a full life, the first step is to have the *courage, commitment* and the *need* to begin the search. It takes *courage* to move from a known position of security, *commitment* to overcome inertia and habit and the *need* to provide the prime motivation for developmental change itself. For reasons discussed earlier, replacing life-diminishing ideas with life-enhancing ones is far easier than identifying them. For many people a startling moment of insight allows for recognition of a false belief and its limitations, and is in itself the beginning of a new vision. This was once described by a student of my Effective Living course as a *"startling awareness that the struggle was over"* and by another that they *"had not found a new path but had removed the major obstacle on the old one."*

How then can you identify these limiting areas? The first step is to develop a deepening personal awareness of the meaning of your personal opinions and values by gently reflecting upon such questions as: What are your "felt" opinions about the major areas of your life? (i.e. ambition, family, life, general values and God). How do you reinforce those opinions? How do you feel? What do you want out of life? I will then look at several ways to get in touch with "these opinions" including a structured process called the S.A.F.E.R method.

Carefully complete the following two exercises. At the end of both are questions that focus on your initial conclusions. *Your answers should reflect how you feel NOW and not how you WANT to feel, SHOULD feel, NEED to feel, or HAVE felt. The first exercise looks at various aspects of your Vision and the second identifies its stronger and weaker areas. The* words given are examples only but you may use them if you wish. It is suggested that you do the exercises on a separate piece of paper.

Exercise #2: The "I" Chart

1. In box #1 name your strongest and most pronounced qualities (either positive or negative). Positive life-enhancing ones on the left and negative life-diminishing ones on the right.

2. In box #'s 2, 3 and 4, give two or three words that describe your general feelings about the statement in each box. (Positive on the left and negative on the right). Note that the box #2 describes how you *think* others see you, *not* how they *do* see you.

3. In box #'s 5 and 6 describe your greatest growth experience and the greatest obstacle to your growth. For example: *Growth:* Marriage, children, successful business. *Obstacles:* Inability to take criticism, procrastination, poor relationships.

4. In box #7 describe your greatest hope. For example: Living in a peaceful community and having loving relationships.

The "I" Chart

Positive		Negative
Clever	I see myself as:	Over-analytical
Courageous		Inflexible
Loyal	1	Stubborn

	I think others see me as:	
Wise		Impetuous
Kind		Aggressive
Smart	2	A Know it all

	I see others (not loved ones) as:	
Fellow travellers		Opponents
Kind		Selfish
Helpful	3	Obstructive

	I see life and the world as:	
An opportunity		An obstacle
Beautiful		Uninspiring
An experience	4	A struggle

My greatest growth experience:

5

The greatest obstacle to my growth:

6

My greatest hope is:

7

QUESTIONS FOR REFLECTION

When you have completed the above *and before moving on*, take some time to think reflectively about your answers and in particular how you feel about the following questions as they relate to each of the boxes you completed.

Are you content with the way you see yourself?

Does the general way you see yourself help or obstruct your life's goals?

Does the way that you think other people see you differ fundamentally from the way you see yourself?

What does this difference tell you about how you present yourself to others and why?

To further your thoughts in this particular area, ask two or three *loving* and *sincere* friends to give you a few words to describe your most pronounced qualities (either negative or positive). Make sure that you ask them to be both honest and objective and that you are able to accept a critical response.

Do their opinions differ from the way you see yourself and do they differ from the way you think others see you? What does this tell you?

The way you see yourself, the way you "think" others see you and how in fact they really do see you, should all be similar for your self-image to be realistic. Is yours realistic?

How do you generally see people who are not loved ones? How does this opinion help/hinder your growth, comfort level and relationships?

Do you see life as generally an opportunity for experience or as a struggle for survival? Beautiful or uninspiring? A challenge or an obstacle? Why do you think this is?

Do you see the material comforts of the world as things to be enjoyed or possessed?

Are there any areas of the "I" chart that you feel limit you from achieving the greatest hope indicated at the bottom of the chart?

As I have mentioned earlier, there are four general areas of your personal Vision that directly affect your growth into the fullness of life. In order of their progressive importance these are: (a) self-esteem and how you see yourself, (b) relationships and how you see other people, (c) how you see the physical world of "things", and finally, (d) your personal relationship with life itself.

The development of each of these depends upon the prior fulfilment of the one that precedes it. It is *only* when you have a strong, unconditionally loving, viable and fully commit-ted Vision of "self" that you are secure enough to reach out in a loving and committed manner to those around you. This then furthers your ability to develop an appropriate value rela-tionship with the world of "things." It is only then that you are equipped to face the challenges and growth experiences of life itself. This process of progressive integration is very effectively described in Abraham Maslows's great book, *Towards a Psy-chology of Being.*

It is the integration of these four areas of self, others, the world and life in an expanding arena of practical application that forms the framework of an effective life and which directs your major decisions. It is this that finally establishes your per-sonal relationship with the spiritual or divine aspect of your nature.

We all have both positive *(life-enhancing)* and negative *(life-diminishing)* areas of our Vision, but it is the positive areas that give us a sense of purpose and fulfilment. It is equally true, however, that the negative areas and their toxic beliefs will frequently sabotage the more positive decisions that we are inclined to make. In the next two chapters I will be looking at the various methods available to you to isolate both the stronger and weaker areas of your vision, enabling you to change the weaker ones. In the latter part of the book I will apply these principles of change to the vision you have in each of these four areas by asking the question: What is an appropriate life-enhancing attitude to self, others, the world and life?

If you observe a difference between the descriptions that will be given and the opinions you hold in the areas identified in the "I" chart and in the "world view" quiz which follows, it is suggested that you can use the principles of Vision Renaissance to explore, analyse and restructure those which are life-diminishing. Let us take a closer look at these areas in order to identify the beliefs that enhance your life and those which limit it.

Please complete the following exercise before proceeding further and only when you have at least two or three hours of quiet time in which to think about its significance.

Exercise #3: Your World View

Your attitudes affect how you feel and act. This exercise will help to identify your beliefs in six major areas: i.e. how you see: *yourself, the way others see you, their actual opinions of you, others, the world and life.*

Each of the two sets of words below is the opposite of the other. The left is the most positive and life-enhancing and the right is the most negative. In front of each indicate a score from 1–10 ranging from a maximum of 10 if you totally agree with the first choice to a minimum of 1 if you totally agree with the second. For example, in the first set below there is a choice between independent and needy. *If you see yourself* as very independent, resourceful and self-reliant most of the time you might give yourself a 9. If you see yourself as generally self-reliant much of the time but with a regular need for supportive assistance you might give yourself a 6. On the other hand, if you see yourself as highly dependent upon others emotionally, socially or economically a lot of the time you might give yourself a 2 or a 3.

This is a test of how positively (high score) or negatively (low score) you see each of the six areas and should reflect what you DO think, not what you SHOULD or would LIKE to think. After finishing all six sections, total the score at the bottom of each section and that will provisionally identify the strongest area of your belief system and your weakest.

(1) I see myself as ...

_____Independent / Needy

_____Determined / Hesitant

_____Caring / Uncaring

_____In control of my life / Not in control

_____Happy / Miserable

_____Responsible / Unreliable

_____ Interesting / Dull and boring

<u>Total</u> ____

(2) I think others see me as ...

_____Strong / Weak

_____ Determined / Hesitant

_____ Caring / Uncaring

_____ In control of my life / Not in control

_____ Happy / Miserable

_____ Responsible / Unreliable

_____ Interesting / Dull and boring

Total ____

(3) Others see me as ...

(This is how others <u>actually</u> see you. Ask the opinion of several friends but only if you can accept any negative opinions).

_____ Strong / Weak

_____ Determined / Hesitant

_____ Caring / Uncaring

_____ In control of my life / Not in control

_____ Happy / Miserable

_____ Responsible / Unreliable

_____ Interesting / Dull and boring

Total ____

(4) I generally see others as being ...

_____ Loyal /Disloyal

_____ Needing love / Not needing to be loved

_____ Similar to me / Basically different to me

_____ Willing to help / Not willing

_____ Trustworthy / Not to be trusted

_____ Generous / Greedy

_____ Caring / Uncaring

Total ___

(5) My life is ...

_____ An adventure / An endurance contest

_____ For enjoying / For conquering

_____ For loving / Controlling

_____ Full of opportunities / Full of obstacles

_____ Actively growing / Passively surviving

_____ Full of inspiration / Empty of excitement

_____ Measured by growing / By obtaining

Total ___

(6) The world and the things in it are ...

_____ Beautiful gifts / Distractions

_____ To be enjoyed / Rejected

_____ To be used / Accumulated

_____ Mine to enjoy / Mine to keep

_____ To be shared / Coveted

_____ Inspiring / Boring

_____ Enjoyments / Possessions

Total ___

When you have completed this exercise, determine the total for each section. If you have been honest with yourself, these totals will provisionally indicate to you your most life-affirming Vision (highest score) and your most limiting one (lowest score). This experience will be furthered if you carefully review the following questions. Write down your answers either in the space provided or preferably in a separate notebook.

(1) Which area is the *most* life-affirming and why do you think this is so? (If possible try to be as specific as possible. For example: information received in the early environment of growth concerning life, people or general experiences).

_____

_____

_____

(2) What do you regularly do that confirms or reinforces this positive part of your vision?

_____

_____

_____

(3) Which is *least* life-affirming (lowest score), and why is this? (If possible try to be as specific as possible. For example: life experiences or information received in formative years).

_____

_____

_____

(4) What do you regularly do that confirms or reinforces this negative part of your Vision?

_____

_____

5) Which specific areas of your personal life have been affected by the influence of this life-diminishing area? (Observable results).

_____

_____

(6) Do #(1) (self-image), #(2) (how you think others see you) and #(3) (how other people actually *do* see you) differ to a large extent? If so, what does that tell you about yourself and how you present yourself? How does that affect the *authenticity* of your relationships?

_____

_____

_____

(7) Do you feel that *your* image of reality with the lowest score directly inhibits *your* ability to grow/love/experience? If so, how?

_____

_____

_____

(8) Do you see yourself in a loving and admiring manner?

_____

(9) If so, what do you do to express and reinforce those feelings? If you do not, in what ways could you express them if you did?

_____

_____

(10) Are there any areas of your Vision that you suspect may prevent you from achieving your greatest hope?" (As described by you in the "I" chart).

_____

_____

_____

Before looking at a more structured way of isolating the weaker areas of your Vision, let us reinforce the initial insights gained from Exercise #2 and Exercise #3.

I have said that within our belief system there are "Attitudes" which direct our emotional and active responses. These are directly responsible for the way we interpret the realities of our life. In other words, health, happiness and success do not depend upon our genes, stars, race, creed or gender but upon what's in our head. *Our emotions and subsequent actions may be stimulated by outside events but they are always created by internal perceptions.*

You might compare the effect of these inner beliefs to the way the inner "seed" of a plant or vegetable affects its shape, texture, taste, and colour. Let us take an onion for example *(Fig# 2)*. If you peel away its outer layers, you will observe that at its centre is an inner "seed" which affects every aspect of its growth and from which that growth develops and emanates. Although this "seed" can never be specifically identified you know that all the onion's characteristics of taste, texture and smell flow from it. We are similar in that we also have "Attitudes" that affect every aspect of *our* life. With this as a personal example *(Fig# 2)*, be a detective and peel through the levels of your own personality to locate the inner "Attitudes" beneath, and in the way that a physician traces back from symptoms to causes, look at the various levels of your own personality and see how they are affected by your internal belief system.

FIGURE # 2

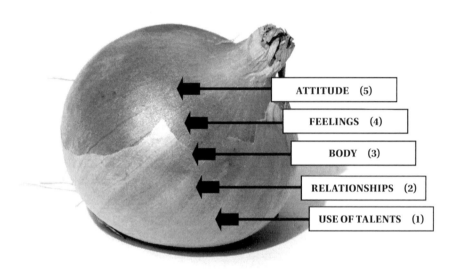

ATTITUDE (5)

FEELINGS (4)

BODY (3)

RELATIONSHIPS (2)

USE OF TALENTS (1)

Let us look at four aspects of your personality:

1) Your talents and abilities and how you discover and develop them.

2) Your relationships and how you create and sustain them.

3) Your body and physical health.

4) Your emotional feelings.

1) Use of Talents

It is said that we all have a special skill, talent or passion that often lies dormant until given the opportunity to grow.

How often do you make a regular and concerted effort to find your skill, talent or passion and then develop it? Do you play it safe, staying in a comfort zone, scared to test your true potential by making excuses to avoid facing the challenge and risk of growth? *"I don't have the time", "It's too expensive", "There are already lots of people doing it", "People don't start to do that at my age."* The list of excuses can be endless, but it is important to remember that they are usually excuses and not reasons.

It has been said that in each person there is a book waiting to be written. Have you thought about writing a book? If you have, have you considered its plot and theme? Have you sat down to actively pursue writing it or perhaps taken lessons in creative writing?

What about playing a musical instrument? Have you ever wanted to play one? Do you realize that if you took one lesson a week and practised solidly for thirty minutes every day for six months, you could master any musical instrument at an introductory level? If you have something that you want to do but have never taken the time to do it, what hidden messages are flowing from your Vision that prevent you from doing so? When you are thinking of stepping out of your personal comfort zone or have actively done so, what self-sabotaging thoughts are trying to stop you? *"What is all this hard work going to get me?" " I'm wasting my time", "It's not been done before", It's been done too many times before", There's no room left for a newcomer."*

If someone you love confides in you that they want to pursue a dream, such as a particular skill, hobby, adventure, career, or private business, what would you do? You would probably encourage, assist and advise them. You would probably try to defeat their fears and objections by providing positive comments and practical help. *Do you do this for yourself? If not, what does this tell you about your own Vision of self and in particular, your degree of self-love?*

One way to defeat the negative comments that affect your efforts is a personal commitment to the process of growth itself rather than to the goal. I have spoken to scores of successful men and women in all walks of life, each of whom have been successful in reaching their own dream. Many have failed several times before doing so, but they all admit to having experienced an empowering moment of commitment when they *knew* they were right and that nothing could or would sidetrack their efforts. A commitment that saw the goal not as a possibility, a dream or even a probability, but as rock-solid reality. The process of moving towards that reality is the glory of committed growth. The secret of commitment is in realizing that we are primarily process-oriented beings not goal-oriented ones (contrary to the suggestion of many motivational "gurus"), and that the intangible state of mind that is called happiness is generally the by-product of meaning and daily purpose rather than actual achievement. For you to concentrate and to agonize *only* upon various aspects of the "worthiness" of a goal is to begin sabotaging your personal growth.

Ask any adult professional when the most meaningful, fulfilling and growth-directed period of their life was, and with few exceptions, they will tell you that it was not when they were finally accepted into medical or law school, when they graduated, or when they were offered their first high-paying job. Nor even when they started to obtain the tangible material benefits of their professional status. Most of them will tell you that it was during their years of hard study, the daily frustration of balancing work and social activities and the ongoing stress of possible failure.

Spend a few minutes making a list of the things that you would very much like to do in the next ten years. Be as specific as you can. Your list can be as long as you like and might well include such things as backpacking through Europe, learning to play the guitar, developing more rewarding and deeper relationships, writing a book, starting a small business in your particular field, learning a second language, taking singing lessons, joining an acting company and taking part in a production or becoming active in a political group. The list is endless, but each item should be something that deep down you think you would like to do and which would call for the development of a specific skill.

Now look carefully at your list and ask yourself how many of those items would have been on a similar list ten years ago. Ten years is a long time to wait. *What reasons did you give yourself in the past for not starting them? Were those reasons factual or just excuses? Why did you use them? What do those answers tell you about your inner vision? Are you still making the same excuses while time is moving relentlessly onward?*

Life calls to each of us in its own way. Sometimes the call is clear and authoritative, but mostly it is quiet and still but none the less compelling in its urgency. The call promises neither pleasure nor pain, as this would be contrary to the laws of balance, but it is, however, a call to live and to be conscious of the breath of life within. It is a call to experience, to feel, to hope, to harmonize, to love and to dream.

How do you recognize when life is calling? Many people have commented that there is often an overwhelming sense that "this is for them" and that they feel a compelling need that manifests itself as a sense of personal anxiety when not fulfilled. In others, it is sometimes more subtle and can be identified only by the careful and subjective answering of questions that reflect upon their needs, dreams and longings. *What did you want to do/be when you were young and why? What did you like to do? What do you dream about? How do you see yourself in your dreams? What were you naturally good at? What characteristics flow through your hobbies? Whom do you admire? Why do you admire them? And what have your friends suggested that you should do?*

In making these observations, do not automatically ignore imaginative childhood dreams, ideas that seem unobtainable or even comments from friends or relatives that may seem self-serving or even manipulative. Sometimes others can see special qualities in us that we tend to ignore.

Your childhood and adolescent dreams and even those in your adult life may indeed appear to be unrealistic, but even at a very young age they are often guides to a much deeper essence of your being. *What is the theme running through those dreams? What are the inner felt pathways they point to? Can they be channelled in other equally fulfilling directions?*

A young man who sees himself as a successful courtroom lawyer, for example, but who does not have the opportunity to become one, may well become a successful motivational speaker or trainer; a man who dreams of being a wealthy industrialist may sublimate those dreams by being a successful realtor; the individual who dreams of being a great politician may work happily at the municipal level of politics or become a community activist and a young person's vision of a successful acting career may be fulfilled within the community theatre. Ultimately, each activity will proclaim in its own unique way, a deeply felt aspiration.

You will in your lifetime have many calls, each of which will represent an aspect of your potential destiny. If you ignore the call, rationalize it too much, let it be sabotaged by your own personal fears, agonize over imaginary and unpredictable consequences, let others tell you how to answer it or play it safe, the calls will get less and less and life will flow out of you. Conversely, if you listen to them and then act upon them, you will be taking the courageous path of true self-knowledge. In doing so you will *definitely* make mistakes, you will *certainly* be criticized and there is no doubt that you will feel both the joy and pain of growth, sometimes even more pain than joy, but at the same time you will begin to see, perhaps for the first time, the glorious highlands of human endeavour and to glimpse the further heights yet to be ascended by the courageous heart.

2) *Your Relationships*

The next level I am going to look at as we continue our journey through the outer layers of our onion is that of relationships. Every psychiatrist and student of human nature will tell you that, for optimum emotional and spiritual health, all individuals need at least one other person with whom they are extremely close, at least one other person to whom they can discuss their problems with total freedom and who will listen objectively to their every fear. Someone they can completely trust and with whom they can be fully authentic. *Do you have such a relationship? If not, does that tell you something about your trust of others, your self-image and your ability or need to communicate? What does it tell you? How easily do you make friends, and more importantly, what happens to those friendships? Do they deepen and become ever more enriched over the years or do they bloom for a short while and then just as quickly wither on the vine? What do you do to enrich and retain your friendships, or do you rely on the other person to keep them going? When your friendships cease, do you react with bitterness? Do you say, "Who cares? I didn't need them anyway." Do you try to repair the breach to the friendship when it has been made or just let things be?*

Human beings are tribal animals with a gregarious instinct which actively seeks the security, camaraderie, support, sense of belonging, personal affirmation and love that friends, family and the group will provide. It is said that no man is an island and those individuals who proudly proclaim themselves as being "loners" and who do not need people often hide an inner pain or fear. What is that fear and what beliefs make you adjust to its pain? Do you feel vulnerable believing that a perceived personal inadequacy may make you weaker, or that others may take advantage of you in some way? If so, what does that tell you about your self-image and your opinion of others? Is it because you believe that others cannot generally be trusted and will hurt you in some way, or that your resources are not sufficient to deal with it if they do? The truth, however, is that most people are the same as you. Equally honest, compassionate, humane, vulnerable, scared and needful of the same love, companionship and acceptance that all of us long for. Why should they not be the same? It is obvious that you cannot be the only virtuous person gifted by nature with these qualities and needs. It is only within an enriching, risk-taking, vulnerability-accepting and eventually loving relationship with others that your own identity can be fully established. I am not referring to a vaguely expressed love for humanity that often hides a hidden agenda of selfishness, but a deeper, more difficult and ultimately more rewarding relationship with those immediately around you. As the English poet G. K. Chesterton put it so effectively in his book, *The Heretics:*

> *"We make our friends, we make our enemies, but God makes our next door neighbour. Hence he comes to us clad in all the careless terrors of nature.*
> *That is why the old religions and the old scriptural language showed so sharp a wisdom when they spoke, not of one's duty towards humanity, but of one's duty towards one's neighbour. Duty towards humanity may take the form of a choice, which is personal or even pleasurable. It may be a hobby or dissipation. We may fight for international peace because we are fond of fighting, not because we are very peaceful and even the most monstrous martyrdom may be the result of selfish choice. But we have to love our neighbours because they are there, a much more alarming reason for a much more serious operation.*
> *God knows that our arms are not big enough to embrace humanity but our neighbours are the sample of it that is actually given to us. Precisely because they may be anybody – they are everybody."*

As we continue through the various layers of the onion to discover our inner beliefs, let us now take a brief look at our physical body and how it is also affected by them.

3) Our Physical Body

Be aware of your bodily feelings both now and in the past (not emotional feelings). Your tensions, headaches, high blood pressure, fatigue and backaches: *What do these tell you about your "attitude?"*

It is said that the body and its physical condition are very clear indicators of the state of your belief system and that your body will physically rebel when forced to adjust unreasonably to an erroneous belief. Karl Menninger, the founder of the Menninger Clinic and one of America's most prominent physicians, suggested that the only "natural" reason for someone to die was when their body parts wear out and that premature death from disease was influenced greatly by life-diminishing rather than life-enhancing beliefs. When your beliefs are generally balanced in favour of life, you will live; when not, you will begin the process of dying.

One unique quality that human beings have is the almost unlimited ability to adjust psychologically to an unfavourable environment. Frequently this adjustment is rationalized by false beliefs as to why there should be no change and the individual's tolerance level is adjusted accordingly. An unhappily married woman, for example may justify her continuance in an abusive relationship by saying to herself, *"As the world outside is a dangerous place, I must put up with my present situation* OR ELSE *I will be in even greater danger."* An intolerable job situation can be justified by thinking, *"I must tolerate my job and its frustrations* OR ELSE *people will think I am a quitter and a loser."* An unadventurous and dull lifestyle can be justified by believing that, *"I must adjust to my present dull and boring lifestyle* OR ELSE *my family (culture/religion) will think any alternative is irresponsible and that would be intolerable."* The defects in logic are obvious but are overlooked by the emotive power of an unchallenged belief, and when believed, lifestyles are adjusted accordingly. Although there are survival advantages in doing this, the serious disadvantage is that your physical body will not always follow this adjustment as willingly. If you adjust too much (and people usually do), the body will rebel and there will be serious physical consequences such as high blood pressure, aches, tensions, fatigue, insomnia, heart disease and cancer.

The sort of self-awareness questions that should be asked here are: *Are you working too hard? Why? Do your reasons justify the sacrifices that you are making? Do you worry too much about trivial matters? Are you able to balance rest/work/play? How easy is it for you to resist being at the "beck and call" of others? Are you living in a life-diminishing situation (marriage, job, relationship)? And are you adjusting to those situations too much? If any of these affect your physical health in some way, why are you doing it? And what statements are you making to yourself that justify or rationalize it?*

4) Feelings

Finally, let us look at your feelings and emotional patterns. *How do you feel right now? Are you happy or sad? What are your general feelings and are you enjoying life? When you wake up do you look to the heavens and say, "Good morning, God" or do you slide out of bed with a groan and say "Good God, it's morning?",* If you're feeling happy and positive about life, take a look at your emotional patterns. *What are you saying to yourself that produces them?* If you're happy, it's a positive indication that your Attitudes to life are healthy, but if you're not, *what is in your Vision that's taking away your joy?*

We all know successful people who are miserable, often without good reason, but equally, we know those who face lives of silent despair with a quiet and dignified resignation that often rises to a joy and happiness that overcomes their pain.

A writer recently described a schoolteacher neighbour who rarely smiled or made a positive comment during the several years he knew her, her face being permanently etched with worry lines. One day she angrily showed him a mean and anonymous note received from one of her students, which read, *"If you're happy, please notify your face."* He was tempted to ask, *"And if you're not, what's in your attitude that drains the joy of life from your veins?"*

On the other hand, one of the most outwardly happy and upbeat people I have ever met looked after the elevator in a large financial institution in England. Bessie was an elderly lady with limited resources who had lost her husband, the father of her two sons, in the First World War. As a single mother, and with great hardship, she brought the two boys up, only to lose both of them in the Second World War twenty-five years later. With limited skills and education, she ended her days as an elevator operator. All who knew her, however, from the boardroom to the mailing room, respected this lady upon whom fate had certainly not smiled kindly.

Bessie saw herself as the first line representative of her organization and her job as a personal mission. She welcomed with a smile everyone who came into the elevator and engaged all her customers, as she called them, in conversation, remembering their names and details of their lives. No one who ever entered "her" elevator remained unaffected by Bessie's earthy philosophy, warm humour, and pithy, down-home advice. When I once asked her the source of her popularity and sense of well-being, she told me that she had a secret. Looking straight at me and being serious just for a moment, she said, *"No power in God's universe can withstand the onslaught of a well-aimed grin."* What was it in her attitude that gave her life meaning and in the other's, frustration?

If you're lonely, sad, depressed, angry or anxious about the future, take a careful look at the Attitudes that govern your emotions and actions. Study them and get to know them and this will help you to find the cause of your pain.

The S.A.F.E.R. Method

In the previous pages of this chapter, I have looked at several general ways of becoming aware of one's limiting beliefs and I hope that a careful review of the "I" chart at the beginning, the answers and conclusions derived from the World View Quiz, and the thoughts developed by going through the layers of the onion will have encouraged you to have an initial awareness of how your own attitudes may affect you.

I will now look at a much more structured approach to locating a specific life-diminishing part of your belief system. I call this the S.A.F.E.R. method, where:

S = Stimulating agent
(An event, word or thought that causes an emotional reaction and a subsequent action)

A = Attitude
(The statement in the "black box" of your Vision that evaluates the stimulating agent described above)

F = Feeling
(The feeling that the above "attitude" created i.e. joy, sadness, frustration, anger, jealousy, etc.)

R = Resultant behaviour
(What you did as a result of the above feeling)

Please do not complete the S.A.F.E.R chart on the next page until you have read __all__ the instruction notes that immediately follow it. The section headed ATTITUDE should not be completed until all other sections are finished.

Exercise#4
The S.A.F.E.R Chart

S = STIMULATING AGENT
(An event, word or thought that causes an emotional reaction and a subsequent action)

_____

_____

_____

↓
A = ATTITUDE
(The statement in the "black box" of your Vision that evaluates the stimulating agent described above)

_____

_____

_____

↓
F = FEELING
(The feeling that the above "attitude" created i.e. joy, sadness, frustration, anger, jealousy, etc.)

_____

_____

↓
R = RESULTANT BEHAVIOUR
(What you did as a result of the above feeling)

_____

_____

_____

Apply this method right now, by using the above S.A.F.E.R. template to look at an *area* of your life which you consider is either (a) not fulfilling, (b) not appropriate to achieving your life's goals, or (c) does not fall within your definition of an effective life. I would suggest that you use a separate notebook to complete the various steps of the exercise rather than the small space in the book itself.

Although it would be extremely helpful for you to have a personal example, it is not absolutely necessary at this stage, as long as you understand the practical application of the exercise in a real life setting and can apply it when the need occurs.

INSTRUCTIONS FOR COMPLETING THE S.A.F.E.R. EXERCISE

(1) As mentioned above, spend some time thinking about an area of your life which is limited or which limits you in some way. You need not be too specific right now but you should try to choose an area that identifies with a regular behaviour pattern. *(For example, I always seem to - -, It seems that I usually - -, When this happens I usually - -, I always get frustrated when - -, I usually get very defensive when - -).* It may help to ask a *loving and objective* friend whose opinion you trust to help you and to confirm your thoughts. It may also help to think in terms of the four areas of your growth patterns: how you see yourself, others, life and the world. Within these areas your concerns may be:

<u>Self:</u> *Lack of confidence, shyness, fear of taking chances, guilt, self-judgemental, lack of joy, feelings of inadequacy, sensitivity to criticism, procrastination, inconsistency, anger, inability to focus.*

<u>Others:</u> *Shallow or short-term relationships, lonely, shy, unreasonable expectations of others, lack of trust, conflict.*

<u>Life:</u> *Decision-making conflict, boredom, worrying about the future, sense of life being unfair/unjust, need to control events,*

frustration when plans are "thwarted", feelings that everything has to be experienced as soon as possible.

<u>The World of "things"</u>: *Need for personal recognition, withdrawal from the world of "things", overly acquisitive, preference for "things" over people (friends, family, obligations).*

(2) Having isolated at least one area, note fully on a separate piece of paper, *using the structure of the S.A.F.E.R. template,* all the details of a recent action(s) that was/were a practical example of the result of that limitation in practice and the resultant feedback those actions produced – "R" on the S.A.F.E.R. chart above. These should be based on what you *did* that you consider inappropriate, and *not* what you *felt*. For example:

"When my boss recently criticized me, <u>I acted defensively</u> and with hostility and spent the rest of the day angry with my staff."
(Sensitivity to criticism)
rather than
"When my boss recently criticized my work, <u>I felt</u> inadequate."

"When I went to the business gathering, <u>I was reserved</u>, stood at the back and <u>didn't speak</u> to anyone."
(Lack of social confidence)
rather than
"When I went to the business gathering, <u>I felt</u> shy and inadequate among all these confident people."

"When a new acquaintance intimated a closer relationship, <u>I acted</u> as though I did not care and was not interested."
(Inability to make close friends)
rather than

"When a new acquaintance intimated a closer relationship, I felt vulnerable and insecure."

"When a friend who had badly hurt my feelings tried to apologize, I continued to hold a grudge and would not accept his apology."
(Inability to forgive)
rather than
"When a friend who had badly hurt my feelings tried to apologize, I still felt angry and resentful and felt like making him feel guilty."

If you choose more than one scenario you will often find, upon examination, that a similar error in perception is common to all of them.

(3) The next step, "S" (Stimulating agent) in the S.A.F.E.R. chart, is to describe in detail the initial event that stimulated the attitude/emotion/action sequence. In the above four examples the descriptions could be: The boss being critical, being at a business meeting, suggestion of a closer relationship and what the friend said or did that was hurtful.

(4) Describe in "F" (Feeling) in the S.A.F.E.R chart the emotion that was *immediately* stimulated by the above event and which caused your subsequent actions, such as anger, frustration, guilt, inadequacy, fear, despair or envy. In the four examples above, those feelings may have been *anger, inadequacy, fear* and *mistrust* respectively.

Do not complete the section headed "ATTITUDE" for the time being

(5) Ask yourself what is the all-important "A" (Attitude) on the S.A.F.E.R. chart that both justified and caused your actions? The *first* step in identifying this Attitude is to create a statement, in the form of those previously indicated, that suggests both (a) what you felt you had to do, and (b) the perceived consequences of not doing so when faced with that particular stimulating agent. There are two aids that I can suggest that will help to do this: Visualization and Verbalization.

VISUALIZATION: Imagine, *in its simplest form*, the picture that immediately arose when the stimulating agent occurred, and if possible draw it. You might, for example, draw a picture of a circle of matchstick men throwing things at you in the centre, or of yourself being overwhelmed by rain and lightning. Of greater importance is for you to capture the overall but *simple* feelings that the situation generated. For example, a picture of chaos might represent lack of control by being overwhelmed by outside circumstances or uncertainty when facing humiliation. Try to see and feel the situation as clearly and as *simplistically* as possible, as if through the eyes of a child.

VERBALIZATION is an extension of visualization in that you try to describe the feelings and visual image with a *simple* expression:

> *"I did the best I could, why don't you like me?"*
> *"I'm scared, I don't know what to do"*
> *"God will not love me"*
> *"I'm scared of you – I want to run away"*
> *"If I'm bad, you'll notice me"*
> *" I want to make everyone happy"*
> *" I don't want to – people may laugh"*
> *" I don't want to go out because it's dangerous"*

The statement must be *as simple* a description as possible. By concentrating on the emotions, actions and images and the simple words they created, you will be able to construct the belief statement that created them. The next step is to then refine the accuracy of the Attitude statement.

Do you mean *must* or *want* to?

Do you mean *all* people or *some* people?

Do you mean *all the time* or *only when* - - -?

For example, you might, if you are overly sensitive to criticism, construct an Attitude statement such as:

"I must be always approved by all those who are significant to me *OR ELSE* I will feel that I have no value."

In regard to this example, do you mean *everyone* or *some people?* (Men, women, people in authority, people you perceive as more intelligent).

Do you mean *must, should be, would like to or need to?*

Do you mean *always, occasionally, in challenging moments, when you have to perform, etc?*

Do you mean *no value, not be in control, in danger or not be loved, etc.?*

When you have specifically isolated an Attitude statement that you *truly believe* created both the emotion and action described in the chart, write it in the appropriate spot (A = Attitude).

(6) The final step is to look carefully, rationally and objectively at the Attitude statement that you have constructed and write down all the reasons that it is *not* a rational and logical interpretation of your *current* reality.

On the next page are three samples of completed charts. Please review them *very carefully* and then complete the previous template for yourself.

Example #1
The S.A.F.E.R. chart
S = STIMULATING AGENT
(Any event that stimulates an emotional response)

My boss was critical of a business report that I had prepared.
↓
A = ATTITUDE
(The Vision statement that evaluates the above. ("Must" or "should" statement qualified by "OR ELSE." Complete later when other parts are finished)

(Visualization): I pictured myself as very small and in danger.
(Verbalization): I'm doing my best, why don't you like me?

I must be approved by people who are significant to me OR ELSE I will have no value.
↓
F = FEELING
(This is the feeling in you that the above Attitude created i.e. joy, sadness, frustration, anger or jealousy)

Anger at being made to feel worthless.
↓
R = RESULTANT BEHAVIOUR
(This is what you did as a result of the above feeling)

I acted defensively, left the office abruptly, was irritable with my staff and started thinking about leaving my job.

In this example, the resultant behaviour was probably inappropriate. Undue sensitivity to criticism is usually self-defeating in the workplace, irrespective of its justification. Beliefs that base self-value solely on exterior approval usually produce inappropriate anger when that approval is not forthcoming.

Example #2
The S.A.F.E.R. chart
S = STIMULATING AGENT
(Any event that stimulates an emotional response)

I stayed late at my boyfriend's office to help him, even though I had previously arranged to meet some friends.
↓
A = ATTITUDE
(Your Vision statement that evaluates the above. ("Must" or "should" statement qualified by "OR ELSE." Complete later when other parts are finished)

(Visualization): Sitting quietly with no one paying me any attention.
(Verbalization): Can I do something so you'll recognize me?

I must be useful to people OR ELSE I will not be loved (lovable).
↓
F = FEELING
(This is the feeling in you that the above attitude created i.e. joy, sadness, frustration, anger, jealousy)

Need to be recognized.
↓
R = RESULTANT BEHAVIOUR
(This is what you did as a result of the above feeling)

Stayed late and helped but felt depressed and used. This caused us to fight as usual.

You need to be loved for your unique personal qualities. When you see yourself as worthy of love only when you are useful, you will attract people who cannot see those qualities and who will use you.

Example # 3
The S.A.F.E.R. chart
S = STIMULATING AGENT
(Any event that stimulates an emotional response)

I asked my husband to explain something to me that I didn't immediately understand.
↓
A = ATTITUDE
(Your Vision statement that evaluates the above. "Must" or "should" statement qualified by "OR ELSE." Complete later when other parts are finished).

(Visualization): A picture of me wandering around lost.
(Verbalization): I need to understand things to be safe.

I must understand and be in control of events and things around me OR ELSE I will be in danger.
↓
F = FEELING
(This is the feeling in you that the above attitude created i.e. joy, sadness, frustration, anger, jealousy)
Inadequacy followed by frustration.
↓
R= RESULTANT BEHAVIOUR
(This is what you did as a result of the above feeling)
When I did not immediately understand I got angry, told him that I was stupid and stormed out of the room.

If not being able to understand something immediately creates feelings of inadequacy, the immediate response to any new learning situation will be either fear followed by escape or anger at a perceived lack of control.

Have you completed the blank S.A.F.E.R chart? If not, please do so now. To give you as much space as possible you should complete it on a separate piece of paper using the S.A.F.E.R. template on page 95 as a guide.

Complete a separate one for each of those areas of your life which are either (a) not fulfilling, (b) not appropriate to your life's goals, or (c) which are not within your definition of an effective life.

Examples might include (but certainly not be limited to): Relationships, procrastination, fear of aging, sensitivity to criticism, lack of drive, boredom and impatience.

The stimulating agent in each example will be a recent event which was typical of that limitation being played out. For example, if you chose procrastination, the stimulating event might be your purposeful and inappropriate delaying of an important project. Sensitivity to criticism might be a bad argument with a spouse initiated by their reproaching you over something quite minor. Relationships might be the final recent event that caused either a full break or a temporary suspension of a close relationship.

The purpose of the exercise is to isolate the subconsciously held Attitudes that stimulate our emotions and inappropriate actions. In the next chapter we will look at ways to change those beliefs.

In the preceding pages of this chapter I have looked at various methods of contacting the beliefs that form part of your "vision" of reality, especially those that prevent you from leading a full and effective life. I am now in a position to move to the second part of the Vision Renaissance method, Attitude reconstruction. Here is a summary of the major points of the preceding chapter.

SUMMARY OF CHAPTER FOUR

1. It takes personal courage to search for limiting Attitudes, to think about them, to question their logic and appropriateness and then to change them. This involves moving from a perceived comfort zone. The process of change starts by being aware of any life-diminishing beliefs that are held, knowing how they were formed and how they affect your life.

2. Completion of the "I" chart begins the process of awareness and completion of the World View Quiz will focus on the stronger and weaker areas of your Vision.

3. A thorough understanding of the theory and practice of the S.A.F.E.R. method will enable you to locate those areas of your Vision that limit you from a full life.

Chapter Five

RECONSTRUCTING YOUR BELIEF SYSTEM

"They always say time changes things, but you actually have to change things yourself."
                                                                    Andy Warhol

"In every moment of your existence you are growing into more or retreating into less."
                                                                    Norman Mailer

"Things do not change; we change."

                                                        Henry David Thoreau

"The noblest within us is brought forth not in contentment but in discontent, not in truce but in fight."
                                                        Baruch Charney Vladeck

"Discontent is the first step in the progress of a man or a nation." Oscar Wilde

"It's not that some people have willpower and some don't. It's that some people are ready to change and others are not."
                                                            James Gordon M.D

"Change has a considerable psychological impact on the human mind. To the fearful it is threatening because it means that things may get worse. To the hopeful it is encouraging because things may get better. To the confident it is inspiring because the challenge exists to make things better."   King Whitney

"You only fail when you fail to dare, not when you dare to fail. God doesn't look at your diplomas, only how you deal with your scars."
                                                                    Anonymous

As previously mentioned, your Vision is composed of specific beliefs (Attitudes), each of which are habitual thought patterns and particular ways of seeing things. Every time you rehearse these, their hold on you becomes deeper and stronger and in the end they will own you. If, for instance, you think and feel that you are a "nobody" and have no importance you will act accordingly. People around you, not knowing any better, will then believe and ultimately confirm that sense of inadequacy by their words and actions. This then becomes the confirming feedback that encourages you to say, "you see, I was right, I am a nobody."

What then can you do to break this cycle once you have become aware of a crippling belief? In this chapter I am going to suggest four habit-making and habit-breaking techniques for personal change. These techniques can only be used *when you have isolated a crippling belief so clearly that you have no possible doubt as to its authenticity and the damage it causes.* It is this assurance and awareness that will give you the commitment to continue. *This is why a sincere and thoughtful attempt must be made to complete the S.A.F.E.R chart in the previous chapter before you proceed further.* As we have discussed earlier, the most important thing to understand is that the development of a life-diminishing belief is maintained by four mutually dependent factors: your thoughts, feelings, actions and feedback, with each one reinforcing the other.

It follows that if you wish to change this pattern you can start with your thoughts *or* your feelings *or* your actions, each being reinforced or weakened by the confirming or negating feedback that you receive. This circular process is the basis of the four techniques of change that I call C.M.E.A. where:

C = Countering
M = Modelling
E = Expanding
A = Affirming

Although these will be described consecutively below, you should endeavour to practise each of them at the same time as they mutually reinforce each other.

C = Countering

This is to be used to counteract the original thought which gave rise to the feelings and actions. It involves looking at the original Attitude and countering it by creating a *logical* and *life-enhancing* statement, which directly challenges the original thought and which can be used to attack it, *even though in the early stages you will not believe the new statement.*

This revised statement is a formidable weapon in your arsenal of change. The statement should be written down (on a small card for example) and put where you will regularly see it. This can be on your desk, in your handbag or wallet, pasted on the bathroom mirror or in the front of the book you read before retiring at night. Its existence should form part of your overall awareness and should be observed and brought to mind *regularly* and *often* so that it becomes a habitual part of your thoughts. Its purpose is to act as a visual focus for change. However, its importance lies *not* in the fact that it is true (as at that moment you do not believe it, even though you may wish to), but in that it begins a process of developmental change that allows the other factors of Modelling (feeling), Expanding (acting) and Affirming (observation of feedback) to begin their magic. Described on the next page are several examples of life-diminishing Attitudes (many of which may affect you in some way) along with typical counter-logics that you may use in this manner.

ATTITUDES AND COUNTER-LOGICS

Attitude	*Counter-logic*
Everyone must approve of me or I will feel like a failure.	The only true failure is not to be open to growth.
I must be useful or else I will not be loved (lovable).	I will be loved if I am honest in expressing who I really am.
I must be happy or else I will feel unjustly treated by life.	I will be happy if my goals include a loving family and friends.
The past made me what I am and therefore I cannot change.	I was born happy and I can make myself happier by the way I think.
I need the approval of others and it's awful when I do not get it.	I desire the approval of others but I do not "need" it.
I must avoid the challenges of life otherwise I will be in danger.	Difficulties are reduced by facing them and increased by avoidance.
I act incorrectly because I cannot control my feelings.	I can control the thoughts that create my feelings.
I must be correct in all my decisions or else I will fail.	Mistakes are part of experience and are proof that I am human.
I need to know and be in control of things or I will be in danger.	As I cannot control the future I will accept unforeseen events.

A counter-logic can be one that fully challenges the illogic of an existing belief, as with those described above, or it can be a short inspirational statement that embraces and proclaims your desired belief. Over the years there have been many of these that have influenced my life and upon which I regularly act. As a young man, for example, I passed through several personal failures. On the occasion of one of these I confided my frustrations to my long-standing family doctor, a man of considerable practical wisdom and much kindness. He questioned me thoughtfully for a few moments and then told me that my problem was not in failing but in not knowing what failure was. *"You only fail when you fail to dare, not when you dare to fail"*, he said quietly and then added, *"God doesn't look at your diplomas, only with how you deal with your scars."* These words, quoted from an unknown source at the right moment, have become one of my most powerful counter-logics to feelings of failure. Whenever, in the intervening years, I have felt discouraged by lack of success I remember those words and they always give me strength.

As a relatively shy individual, whenever I meet people for the first time or am challenged by a difficult personal encounter, I remember Bessie, the elevator operator and the counter-logic that helped her so much, *"No power on earth can resist the onslaught of a well-aimed grin."* Perhaps there are some powers that can, but not many.

A popular writer on human relationships once related the story of how as a young man he was counselling a very troubled and difficult young woman. He mentioned his frustration to a friend, a professional counsellor, who asked whether he had ever had a really bad toothache. When the young man replied in the affirmative, he was asked what was on his mind during this time. The answer, of course, was himself and his pain. The friend then pointed out that the girl was in pain, not physically of course, but in pain nonetheless and unless that was acknowledged and understood by those dealing with her, no progress could ever be made. *"Did you ever have a toothache?"* has become one of my most powerful counter-logics in dealing with people. Whenever I meet an obnoxious or particularly unreasonable individual and before I judge them too harshly, I remember, *"Did you ever have a toothache?"* This does not solve the problem, of course, but by reminding myself that the other person may have an emotional pain or an unresolved conflict, the focus automatically transfers from confrontation and argument to understanding and compassion.

Try it yourself and you will observe a dramatic and positive change in awareness. Many years ago I had a good friend who always acted kindly every morning to a local news vendor who was, in his turn, aggressive and bad-tempered. *"Don't you get angry and want to sometimes tear a strip off that miserable old devil?"* I asked him. *"No,"* was his reply, *"I'm not going to let a miserable old coot like that dictate how I should act, I'm an actor, not a reactor."* I'm an actor, not a reactor. What a wonderful and life-enhancing response to the many daily difficulties we regularly face in life and which are so often beyond our immediate control. *You* decide how you should act. Not the traffic jam, delayed subway or inconvenient weather, but *you*. Your reaction should lead to one rational question. Can you do anything about the problem? And if you cannot, what is the most beneficial way to accept it?

Dealing with difficulties involves deciding whether they are p*roblems* or s*ituations* and responding to them proactively rather than reactively. Recognising the difference is important, as the solution to each requires vitally different skills. *A difficult problem is one that has a solution,* which is why it is described as such and it can be solved by thought, planning, significant effort or by giving up something. A low-paying job, an unhappy marriage or a lonely life are examples of problems that can be solved.

Conversely, *a difficult situation does not have a solution* and therefore needs maturity, endurance and strength of character to accept. Gradual aging, a disability, or in some cultures, one's gender, race or religion may well be difficult and sometimes full of anguish but they are not problems so much as unpleasant situations, the endurance of which may require strength and courage. The problem of course may be how you see those areas of your life and the behaviours you have developed by seeing them that way. If you try to solve a problem merely by adjusting to it, or by endurance or non-action, you will be unhappy and may probably get sick. If you try to solve a situation by overt action, you will probably get frustrated at the lack of change.

Construct appropriate counter-logics which directly challenge the self-defeating *illogic* of an erroneous belief and use them regularly. Keep them fresh and at the forefront of your mind, put them on notes around your bedroom, bathroom or office and think about them before you fall asleep and when you wake up. Eventually, their life-giving message will filter down to the deeper levels of your subconscious mind where they will begin the magical process of reconstruction.

M = Modelling

Modelling is a method of changing the feelings that are created by pre-programmed beliefs. If you have started to positively counter your previous beliefs, those feelings would have started to change already. Feelings will always follow your thoughts in the same way that a glove will follow the movement of your hand. If you move your fingers your glove *will* follow, it cannot do otherwise. If you change your thoughts, your emotions and feelings *will* follow, they too have no choice. If countering, as mentioned above, is a method of changing your thought patterns, modelling is a process of taking this one step further and actively changing your feelings.

Have you ever been to a movie and observed a character that you strongly admire and whose qualities you would like to emulate? Someone whose style, attitude or beliefs resonate within you so that without consciously realizing it, you say to yourself, *"Oh, how I would like to be like that person."* It may be something quite superficial such as admiring the way they order a meal or a drink in a restaurant or their personal charm, or it may be something more subtle, such as their easy manner, their self-confidence, their way of talking to strangers, or of facing and solving a problem. When you leave the theatre and if the character impressed you sufficiently, you may walk around for a few days with their image lingering in your mind. You may start to feel and act a little like that person and if these feelings and actions are not sabotaged by personal habit, you begin to do this more regularly. If you persist with these small changes to your behaviour, your feelings and thoughts will also change to reflect those of your model.

What you are practising here is a very powerful method of change called *introjection,* that is defined in modern psychology as *"the unconscious adoption of the ideas, attitudes or behaviour of others."* Modelling carries this one step further and applies it in a structured and intentional manner to reinforce your changing thought patterns. Having positively identified those personal limitations that hinder growth and having constructed counter-logics that challenge the thoughts that produced them, modelling involves identifying an individual or individuals, alive or dead, real or fictitious, relative, friend or acquaintance who exemplify the qualities you admire. Modelling means becoming aware of their attitudes, feelings and belief structures and how you think they would deal with the various limitations that you face. It means getting into the head of your model and asking, *"How would they have dealt with this issue? What would their feelings have been at this moment? How would they respond?* John Powell, the Jesuit writer, once told of a friend who was in the caring profession and who became burned out because of his inability to say *"No!"* to the various and frequent demands upon his time. One day, upon hearing a friend easily and without explanation decline an inconvenient request, he asked for his photograph, and having written on it a large "NO" placed it next to his phone as a permanent example of his model's ability to decline a request without guilt or excuse.

One of my own limitations has often been a need to compromise with the opinion of a group rather than risk unpopular opposition. The model that has significantly helped me to overcome this is Sir Winston Churchill, Britain's pugnacious wartime leader who embodied the ability to stand fast in defence of his own well thought-out opinions, even at the risk of unpopularity. I have a large, scowling picture of this great man on my living room wall. An individual who is short on compassion and understanding and troubled by a "short fuse" might choose the gentle tolerance and patience of Gandhi. A close friend, a successful man who failed many times in business before finally succeeding, has Abraham Lincoln as his model, a man whose consistent record of electoral failure did not discourage him from becoming one of the most beloved presidents of the United States. Finally, let us not forget the greatest model in the Christian world, Jesus Christ, the gentle reformer from Galilee whose example provides a model for millions.

Modelling means both falling asleep and waking up with an image in your mind that embodies your ideals, not in an obsessive manner but as a guide that will influence your thoughts, feelings and actions. If you feel like doing so, put a picture of your model on the wall, bedside table or sideboard where you can see it regularly and keep it at the forefront of your awareness.

Having identified some of the feelings associated with your new counter-logic, the second part of modelling is to use your imagination to experience those feelings as *realistically* and as *vividly* as possible in an imagined and positive situation. The best time to do this is when you are relaxed and in what is referred to as an "Alpha" state. To understand why this is, it helps to understand the complex relationship between your conscious mind and that of your subconscious mind where your thoughts, memories, attitudes, beliefs and motivations are stored. Your conscious mind implements your daily decisions but it is your subconscious mind that acts as your operating programme and which motivates those decisions.

It has been shown that the brain's ability to receive and convey information to the subconscious mind is largely influenced by the level of its electromagnetic activity, as measured by its wave frequency on an EEG machine. There are four decreasing levels of this frequency: beta, alpha, theta and delta. The fastest of these is beta, which is the level most closely associated with your conscious waking state. This is followed by alpha, a relaxed level bordering on deep sleep, and then by theta and delta, which are progressively deeper levels such as those experienced by medically-induced anaesthesia or when in a coma. Research has shown that the alpha state is closely associated with meditation and hypnosis. Significant evidence supports the belief that when you are at this level, physical and mental capacities are rejuvenated and the subconscious mind is most open to suggestion. It has been shown for example that you are as much as twenty-one times more open to life-changing ideas whilst in this state of consciousness than when you are either fully awake or asleep. The reason for this is not understood but it has been suggested that when the brain is in the alpha state the conscious mind, which normally acts as a filter to resist outward suggestions of unwanted or unjustified change, is "turned off," and in the lower levels of theta and delta those suggestions cannot be received. *The alpha level appears to be that level of consciousness that allows the subconscious mind to directly receive and store life-changing input.* In order to understand the importance, whilst in the "Alpha" state, of vividly imagining the feelings associated with new beliefs, it has to be realized that the subconscious mind operates under two significant parameters. If you understand their significance, and if you practise that understanding, your life will change forever.

1. The subconscious mind cannot distinguish between a real or imagined experience. If thoughts, imaginary emotions and the pictures that accompany them are vividly felt and seen, your mind will accept the beliefs that arise from them as real.

2. The subconscious mind is non-judgemental and does not distinguish between a life-diminishing or life-enhancing input.

What this means is that if something is imagined strongly enough, it will be recorded as a real experience and eventually your life will be directed by the beliefs arising from it, even if those beliefs are negative or life-diminishing. Those beliefs can lead to failure and despair just as effectively as they can lead to success and happiness. The above two principles are at the heart of any philosophy of personal growth.

"The thing always happens that you really believe in."

Frank L. Wright

"They can conquer who believe they can."   *Virgil*

"Believe it can be done. When you believe something can be done, your mind will find ways to do it."   *David Schwartz*

"A man's life consists of what he thinks about all day long."

Ralph Waldo Emerson

"Our life is what our thoughts make of it."   *Marcus Aurelias*

"Thoughts create grooves in our mind, which respond to the great law of habit. Think of your mind as a pliable, plastic surface. When you think the same thought persistently, it cuts an ever-deepening groove, until it becomes like a wagon rut in a country road. Our thoughts then habitually slip into these grooves irrespective of whether they are good or bad, negative or positive."

M. D. Hannah

"The conscious mind is where we reason, select or reject what "seems" to be good or bad. What our reasoned judgement dwells upon sinks into the unconscious mind and becomes part of us. If we think about truth, goodness and beauty, we will build integrated lives. If we indulge in negative thinking we become unhappy and fear-ridden."   *L.L . Dunnington*

"You are today where yesterday's thoughts have brought you; you will be tomorrow where today's thoughts will take you."

James Allen

The alpha state can be reached in various ways. For example, the first moments when you awake and before you have a full awareness of the day, just before you fall asleep, during meditation, after intense exercise and while listening to certain types of mood-inducing and relaxing music, all are times when it is possible to be in the alpha state. A particularly effective method is to look intently for about five seconds at the light bulb in your bedside table lamp (do so cautiously and if you do not have an eye defect that prevents you from doing so). Then lay back and close your eyes. What you will "see" is the circular outline of the bulb, rather like a miniature sun. This is, of course, nothing more than a retinal image. However, after a few moments, it will weaken and disappear, but it can then be easily "willed" back by an effort of concentration where it will usually appear as a sharp blue orb. If you cease concentration and allow your mind to drift, it will disappear. While the "orb" is seen, you are in an alpha state as it is only by concentrating on the orb itself, rather than other things, that the image is kept. It is at this point that the subconscious mind is most receptive to positive input such as affirmations, feelings, and mind pictures. A particularly powerful affirmation that I frequently use is the following ancient Indian prayer taken from the Vedantic tradition and translated from Sanskrit.

"From this day forward I shall become more and more conscious of all that is positive, happy, calming and cheerful. The thoughts that enter my mind will be strong and healthy ones. I shall gain daily in self-confidence and shall believe in my own powers and these will manifest themselves in ever-increasing strength. In a short period of time all the problems that used to perplex me will have vanished and will never return."

E = Expanding

As mentioned previously, each aspect of the C.M.E.A. method (countering, modelling, expanding and affirming) reinforces the others, and because of this you can begin the process of change anywhere on the self-development spectrum of thought, feeling or action, depending upon your own preference and personality.

I will now look at changing the actions that automatically flow from your pre-programmed beliefs, bearing in mind that if you have started the process of countering and modelling, you would have started to change those actions already. Have you noticed how very difficult it is to change habitual actions? This is because you have a built-in psychological resistance to change (especially dramatic change). Any change is seen as risky, even though it may ultimately be for the better. Quite frequently you intentionally sabotage the process of change by "all or nothing" thinking. *"I have to lose 20 lbs in the next 3 weeks"*, (knowing that it is probably impossible); *"I will be the life and soul of the next party and overcome my inhibitions"*, (knowing that you will never have the courage to do it in the way you propose); *"I will purposely not get irritated next time someone badly criticizes me"*, (knowing that your sensitivity is such that you will not be able to avoid it). The subconscious intention here is very often to avoid change rather than to implement it. *The secret of positive change is to take it in small, easy to manage steps.* As each step gets stronger, an increasing awareness is developed and you realize that the new action is not necessarily a hindrance to survival, but may actually enhance it. This increasing awareness is reinforced by affirming and more positive feedback, which in turn strengthens the counter-logic and the feelings it has produced.

Many people are desperately afraid of public speaking. The finest communication training organization in the world – Toastmasters International – recognizes this and conducts its developmental programme accordingly. Guests and new members do not have to participate but are gently encouraged to make a few comments at the end of a meeting. What they do not real-ize, even at this early stage, is that once they have done so, the ice has been broken and they have indeed spoken spontaneously to a group of strangers. Later, they take part in a one-minute spon-taneous speaking exercise that leads very gradually to more complex presentations. Each time, the speaker is complimented on the positive points in their delivery, thus building the self-confidence that facilitates the emergence of their natural ability. These compliments become the affirming feedback that weak-ens the original message that they could not speak in public, and replaces it by a new one that says they can.

A shy person, fearful of new social encounters and equipped with a positive counter-logic and a model, may well enter the next social encounter with one small mission (for example, to start a simple conversation with at least three different people). Not an interesting conversation (too judgemental), not a long conversa-tion (too challenging and possibly self-sabotaging), and certainly not a conversation directed to a specific goal (to appear charming or to get a date). The mandate is *only to start* the conversation, a relatively easy mission.

An employee who is unreasonably sensitive to criticism may make their initial goal to look actively and with awareness for the next situation in which they are criticized. Then, having observed the situation, plan to say, *"I don't quite understand why that irri-tates you. It would really help me if you could discuss it with me,"* or *"Can we look into the matter just a little more deeply?"* or *"Thank you for pointing that out to me but I did the best I could and I'd really appreciate it if you would kindly let me know how I could have done better."* Then, if they felt so inclined, they could become annoyed and respond as they normally would. The point, how-ever, is that they would probably *not* do so, as they would have broken the old reinforcing cycle and would have begun the pro-cess of creating a new pattern of growth.

An individual plagued by grudges and an inability to over-come resentment from previous hurts may choose an individual against whom they harbour a grudge and make their expanding goal a simple smile and a *"Good morning, how are you?"* next time they meet, and to continue smiling, irrespective of the response.

Even though the actions in the above four examples are small ones and will not immediately defeat the underlying belief, they will slowly weaken and eventually replace it.

Expanding involves looking at and understanding the type of fear that cripples you and responding to it ruthlessly with the greatest weapon that you have, ACTION. Note that I only refer to a certain type of fear, because natural fear is a friend not an enemy. Without a healthy fear of real danger you would not survive. You see real danger and you run away from it or fight it.

In this context, "fear" is an immediate feeling followed by an action. Many of life's depressing problems are seldom "real" in this sense and are the product of the imagination. The fear that prevents the achieving of a full and effective life is not fear of the event, but a fear of fear, something I like to call "funk." Funk creates a static source of inaction that prevents growth. This is the fear that becomes poisonous, saps your strength and makes you sick and neurotic. The great psychologist Carl Jung described this well by saying *"Neurosis is man's substitute for legitimate suffering."* In layman's terms, he was implying that when you try too hard to avoid the inevitable pain of growth, and the natural fear that facing it would cause, you become sick. Worry and anxiety are usually due to feelings of inadequacy in coping with the difficulties of life, but these can usually be eradicated by taking firm action, cautious though it may be. If you act, stretch and expand, hope, faith and courage will be reborn.

A = Affirming

It is vital to observe the affirming feedback that you receive as a result of your new way of behaving. This is both internal – *"How do I now feel?"* and external – *"What did I see, hear and experience?"* These observations involve an awareness of how the affirming feedback to your new behaviour patterns compares to the old and the extent to which it enhances or fails to enhance your life.

In the above four examples, the cautious public speaker might observe their feelings before speaking and after having received comments from the audience subsequent to speaking. They will know whether their actual fear was as bad as their anticipated fear, whether they would like to do it again and whether any mistakes were as "catastrophic" as they originally thought they might be. Generally it is "catastrophe" thinking that distinguishes "funk" from healthy caution.

The shy person might observe whether their original fears were justified, the positive responses from the person they spoke to and whether they could do it again.

The over-sensitive employee might look for signs of approval from their boss, a greater understanding of their opinion or enhanced feelings of personal well-being.

The grudge-holder might look for signs of a warmer response, a more trusting relationship or greater feelings of security and comfort in the relationship.

It is important to describe the type of feedback you are looking for at this stage of C.M.E.A. because this supplies the practical proof (limited though it may be in the early stages) that your new thoughts, counter-logics, models, feelings and actions are appropriate to your life and goals. I have shown on the next page a blank C.M.E.A. worksheet and three examples of how it might be completed for the three S.A.F.E.R. examples previously given, so that you may observe the complete process before practising it yourself. The three examples once again are:

- The over-sensitive employee responding angrily to a critical boss.
- A frustrated response to a boyfriend's inconvenient request for help.
- Annoyance felt by an individual at their inability to understand something.

The C.M.E.A. chart

C = COUNTERING

(A positive, life-enhancing and true statement that challenges the goals and logic of an existing identified attitude)

↓

M = MODELLING

(How you will try to experience and imagine the feelings and actions associated with your new attitude and, if possible, a person who practises those feelings and actions)

↓

E = EXPANDING

(The initial progressive actions that you will undertake resulting from the above counter-logic and feelings)

↓

A = AFFIRMING FEEDBACK

(The feedback that will confirm that the counter-logic, modelling and actions above are life-affirming and helpful to your growth and goals)

Example #1

S = STIMULATING AGENT

(Any event that stimulates an emotional response and a subsequent action)

My boss criticized a business report that I had prepared.

↓

A = ATTITUDE

(The statement that evaluates the above. "Must" or "should" statement qualified by" OR ELSE." Complete when other parts are finished)

Visualization: I pictured myself as very small and in danger.

Verbalization: I'm doing the best I can, why don't you like me?

I must be approved by people who are significant to me OR ELSE I will have no value.

↓

F = FEELING

(This is the feeling in you that the above attitude created, i.e. joy, sadness, frustration, anger, jealousy etc.)

I felt anger at being made to feel worthless.

↓

R = RESULTANT BEHAVIOUR

(This is what you did as a result of the above feeling)

I acted defensively, left the office abruptly, was irritable with my staff and started thinking about leaving the job.

Example # 1. Completion of the above.

C = COUNTERING

(A positive life-enhancing and true statement that challenges the logic of the old attitude)

I will have value and will be a success if I allow myself to be open to growth and receptive to the opinion of others.

↓

M = MODELLING

(How you will try to experience and imagine the feelings and actions associated with your new attitude and, if possible a person who practises those feelings and actions)

Every morning I will try to vividly experience feelings of growth, expansion and development. My model is Nelson Mandela growing from revolutionary to world statesman, and I will think about what he would do in situations that make me angry. I will also imagine a rose growing from a bud to full bloom and will carry these thoughts, feelings and those of an enquiring mind daily into the office.

↓

E = EXPANDING

(The initial and progressive actions that you will undertake resulting from the above counter-logic and feelings)

I will keep my new "counter-logic" on my desk and will look for the next time I am criticized so that I can use it. In spite of my irritation, I will apologize and then enquire sincerely as to where I went wrong.

↓

A = AFFIRMING FEEDBACK

(The feedback that will confirm that the counter-logic, modelling and actions above are life-affirming and helpful to your growth and goals)

I will look for and carefully observe my boss's reactions and my own feelings for the rest of the day, to see whether what I did appeared to make sense and whether physically I felt more or less relaxed.

Example # 2.

S = STIMULATING AGENT

(Any event that stimulates an emotional response and a subsequent action)

My boyfriend asked me to stay late at his office to help him, even though I had previously arranged to meet some friends.

↓

A = ATTITUDE

(The statement that evaluates the above. "Must" or "should" statement qualified by "OR ELSE." Complete when other parts are finished)

Visualization: Sitting quietly and insignificantly on a chesterfield, hands in my lap and no one paying attention.

Verbalization: Can I do something so that you'll recognize me?

I must be useful to people OR ELSE I will not be loved (lovable).

↓

F = FEELING

(This is the feeling in you that the above attitude created, i.e. joy, sadness, frustration, anger, jealousy etc.)

I felt a need to be recognized as having value.

↓

R = RESULTANT BEHAVIOUR

(This is what you did as a result of the above feeling)

I agree to help him but felt depressed and used and we argued as usual.

Example # 2. Completion of the above.

C = COUNTERING

(A positive life-enhancing and true statement that challenges the goals and logic of the old attitude)

I am lovable for who and what I am and I will be genuinely loved if I express my emotions and needs clearly and courteously.

↓

M = MODELLING

(How you will try to experience and imagine the feelings and actions associated with your new attitude and, if possible, a person who practises those feelings and actions)

Maria says "No" easily and without excuses to inconvenient requests. I will ask how she feels when doing so and will try to copy those feelings. I will keep her photograph with "No" written on the front and my counter-logic on the back, will think about it daily and will imagine various situations in which I say, "No" easily and without excuse.

↓

E = EXPANDING

(The initial progressive actions that you will undertake resulting from the above counter-logic and feelings)

For one month, when asked to do anything significant, I will respond with, "Let me think about it and I'll get back to you." Then, if the request is not convenient, I will politely say, "No, I can't make it, but perhaps another time." I will be friendly but will not explain.

↓

A = AFFIRMING FEEDBACK

(The feedback that will confirm that the counter-logic, modelling and actions above are life-affirming and helpful to your growth and goals)

I will look for the reactions of those whose requests I reject. I will think about the value of the "friends" whose reactions are negative and will observe whether I feel stronger and less upset when saying "No."

Example # 3.

S = STIMULATING AGENT

(Any event that stimulates an emotional response and subsequent action)

I asked my husband to explain something to me that I didn't immediately understand.

↓

A = ATTITUDE

(The statement that evaluates the above. "Must" or "should" statement qualified by "OR ELSE." Complete when other parts are finished)

Visualization: A picture of me wandering around in a park lost.

Verbalization: I need to understand things in order to be in control and to be safe.

I must understand and be in control of things around me as much as possible OR ELSE I will be in danger.

↓

F = FEELING

(This is the feeling in you that the above attitude created, i.e. joy, sadness, frustration, anger, jealousy etc.)

I felt panic followed by frustration.

↓

R = RESULTANT BEHAVIOUR

(This is what you did as a result of the above feeling)

I got immediately angry, told him that I was stupid and didn't understand anything, and stormed out of the room.

Example #3. Completion of the above.

C = COUNTERING

(A positive life-enhancing and true statement that challenges the goals and logic of the old attitude)

As I cannot predict the future, I will protect my interests by making calm decisions based on available information and will accept the result as a necessary part of living.

↓

M = MODELLING

(How you will try to experience and imagine the feelings and actions associated with your new attitude and if possible, a person who practises them)

I will try to emulate two models. A successful man who accepts the potentially negative results of his many business risks with peace of mind and a friend who has had several successful and unsuccessful careers. I'll try to understand their feelings about challenge and failure. I will imagine moving from my comfort zone into potentially difficult areas and also ways of solving those potential problems.

↓

E = EXPANDING

(The initial progressive actions that you will undertake resulting from the above counter-logic and feelings)

I will engage in some immediate activities that involve a small departure from my comfort zone, and in doing so, will worry less about the results.

↓

A = AFFIRMING FEED BACK

(The feedback that will confirm that the counter-logic, modelling and actions above are life-affirming and helpful to your growth and goals)

I will observe and record the feelings that arise from the above actions and how I reacted to any unforeseen events that occurred.

To summarize how this might work in a practical setting, let us describe an individual who is sensitive to criticism. John, a skilled and well-qualified financial analyst, has worked for five different companies in the last twelve years, each time moving to a similar position. In each, he quickly begins to feel that his personal skills are not recognized and that his immediate superiors are not very competent. This often results in his resenting their constructive comments regarding his performance, which he interprets as unwarranted criticism. He then soon thinks about moving on to a different company. John feels that by now he should have reached a greater level of responsibility and suspects that his frequent moves are beginning to make him look unreliable. John's awareness that he may be reaching a plateau where he is becoming unemployable is the catalyst that forces him to think about his attitude to work and the criticism that can be received.

By practising the two processes mentioned above (S.A.F.E.R. and C.M.E.A)., John decides to take a much more constructive, receptive and open approach to criticism, *not really believing it will work.* He observes quite quickly that the boss's reaction is a *little less* defensive and more cooperative than before, that John's personally felt frustrations upon leaving the office are a *little* better and he begins to think that there may be a degree of validity to the boss's critical comments. Not only does this provide him with additional motivation to continue, but also the feedback supports the validity of his newly formed "attitude." These in turn strengthen the emotions and actions of growth that accompany it. The increased friendliness of the boss and his desire to help inevitably develop cooperation rather than resentment, and this again becomes part of the ever-strengthening cycle of reinforcing feedback $\rightarrow$ attitude $\rightarrow$ feeling $\rightarrow$ action $\rightarrow$ reinforcing feedback.

A point is eventually reached where it becomes obvious at both the conscious and subconscious levels of thought that the original survival message, *"I have to actively protect myself against challenges to my value"* is seen as inappropriate. It is then safely replaced by a new one which maintains that survival and value now depend not on exterior and uncontrollable approval factors, but on an internally controllable and expressed openness to growth. In the Greek Socratic tradition the word for this type of transition was *Metanoia,* meaning a change in one's way of life due to a spiritual, rational or emotional conversion.

SUMMARY OF CHAPTER FIVE

1. Often the mere recognition of a crippling belief is sufficient to begin a process of internal healing.

2. Once a false or limiting belief has been clearly recognized, the C.M.E.A method should be used to initiate the process of healing and change.

3. The first step – countering – involves constructing a counter-logic which weakens the previous attitude and focuses on positive change.

4. The second step – modelling – involves the regular practice of experiencing the feelings associated with your new logic by modelling someone who acts as you would like to and by realistically recreating those feelings.

5. The third step – expanding – involves the gradual and progressive practice of those actions which would logically flow from both the new attitude and the newly experienced feelings.

6. The fourth step – affirming feedback – involves actively observing the feedback received from practising your countering, modelling and expanding techniques. This feedback includes personal feelings of comfort (both emotional and physical), your sense of harmony with the outside world, reduced conflict and improved personal relationships.

Chapter Six

LIVING WITH YOURSELF

"What you think of yourself is much more important than what others think of you."
                                                                          Seneca

"We are so much accustomed to disguise ourselves to others, that at length we disguise ourselves to ourselves."   *Francois Rochefoucauld*

"By despising himself too much a man comes to be worthy of his own contempt."   *Henri Frederic Amiel*

"In everyone's life there comes a time when they have to take themselves lovingly, deeply and passionately into their own arms."   *George Bernard Shaw*

"To be a truly self-caring person is not a negotiable item. To accept ourselves without criticism, blame, denial or guilt is to live with the idea that our identities are intact and worthy of our love. True maturity is the process of testing the self on ever-increasing distances from perceived safety. The upshot is the wonderful freedom we call autonomy."   *Dr. Christopher McCullough*

"The first affair that we must consummate successfully is the love affair with ourselves. Only then are we ready for other love relationships. Ultimately, no matter how concerned we are about others we must be primarily responsible for ourselves, for it is only what we have that we are able to give to another. If we feel inadequate or victimized then we have no power to give another visibility, security and strength. To learn about oneself requires constant awareness of self. It suggests a commitment to the unlimited powers of mind and body to change in a voluntary direction. It involves the termination of self-depreciation and self-deception and observing as best we can how we act out what we believe. Only those who are dedicated to knowing and accepting themselves can accept these qualities in others."   *Nathaniel Brandon*

We have already learned that a personal vision consists of four progressive areas (self, others, the world and life) and that when these are fully integrated they provide the framework for a truly effective life. It is vital, however, that this framework be based on an authentic interpretation of personal reality that is appropriate to growth, well-being and wholeness.

The most important part of this interpretation is the way in which you see yourself, because everything that you do, everything that you feel, every relationship upon which you embark, everything that you experience and every risk that you take is initially filtered through your vision of self. It is therefore imperative that the way you see yourself is based on an authentic, positive and unconditionally loved self-image, because that is the only way to develop high self-esteem. It is only when your vision of self is secure in these areas that you are able and free to step out of the painful insecurity of self-protection and embrace the world as it is. In his book, *The Psychology of Romantic Love*, Nathaniel Brandon wisely suggests that, "There is no value judgement more important to individuals and no factor more important in their psychological development and motivation than the estimate they pass upon themselves."

Many people confuse "self-image" and "self-esteem." It is important that you understand the difference because it is your self-esteem that invariably flows *from* your self-image and subsequently has a great effect upon your capacity to genuinely love yourself.

Self-image is a kind of mentally held collection of pictures of oneself in various situations and at various times in one's life, in the past, present and future. These pictures form a kind of continuously moving collage or movie album that represents a "felt" sense of who you are.

Self-esteem, on the other hand, always implies an element of judgement and emerges when you begin to interpret the set of pictures known as your self-image. It is this all-important judgement factor which can be both critical and harsh or understanding and encouraging, that creates in you the personal sense of your own "niceness" or lack of it, which you grow to love or despise.

If your capacity for self-love emerges from the judgement you apply to your self-image, it is not only obvious that your judgement should be life-enhancing but that you see clearly the difference between the selfishness which results from harsh and critical self-judgement and the self-love that comes from a kinder one. You can do very little to change the reality of the pictures that you have of yourself but you can do a great deal to change the self-esteem that flows from your judgement of them. A high self-esteem will give you the self-confidence to face life, other people and your daily challenges effectively. A low self-esteem will invariably result in such painful limitations of character as hypersensitivity, indecisiveness, perfectionism, inflexibility, non-expression of emotions, dogmatism, a compulsive need to please others and often a smouldering resentment against those who are seen as "better".

In addition to the common confusion between self-image and self-esteem, there is an equally held confusion between self-love and selfishness. Unfortunately, there is in many religions a fundamental belief that self-love is wrong and that even at its best it represents a subtle form of selfishness to be avoided. That if you have too much self-love it will automatically turn into selfishness. These beliefs endeavour to promote an ideal of altruistic self-sacrifice that puts personal interest last in a kind of self-imposed martyrdom. Indeed the ideal of the Christian faith itself is the martyr who died for our sins. I believe that this is not only contrary to the original teachings of the founder of Christianity but to all the tenets of human biology.

Selfishness and self-love are on *opposite* sides of the spectrum of human growth. Erich Fromm, in his wonderful book *The Art of Loving*, remarks that "The selfish person does not love himself too much but too little, in fact he hates himself." The person who is truly self-loving is free from the nightmare of self-protection and can truly reach out and embrace the world and those within it. Selfishness, on the other hand, is not a product of self-love but of self-contempt for our imagined inadequacy which can manifest in many different and sometimes obscure ways. These often include an exaggerated need for self-protection and the need to reduce others to the same level of equalized disdain by criticism, put-down and control. Very often the self-sacrifice that appears to be made on the altar of a noble ideal is not so much an expression of love for the ideal but a desire to eliminate a self that has become unacceptable. Traditionally we are taught to *"Love thy neighbour as thyself."* I believe that if many of us loved our neighbours as we love ourselves, most of our neighbours would be in very serious trouble.

Why is it of such vital importance in the framework of affirming an authentic identity that you become unconditionally self-loving? It is because you project that image to others and it is that to which others respond. *The way others determine who you are and how they should act towards you is based solely on what you tell them about yourself.*

How then can you develop a genuinely and unconditionally loving vision of self, especially if it does not currently exist? In the Vision Renaissance matrix there are two methods to consider. The first is to develop an awareness of what it means to be self-loving and the second is a powerful set of exercises that uses the environment around you to confirm that you are indeed lovable.

Let us look first at what it means to be self-loving and how an unconditionally loving self-image can be developed. I believe that a significant clue is given to us in the traditional injunction mentioned above, *"Love thy neighbour as thyself."* I believe that this strongly implies that you must love yourself *before* you can love your neighbour, or put another way, you cannot love your neighbour *unless* you love yourself first.

Let us, however, reverse this for a moment i.e. *"Love yourself as you love your neighbour"* rather than *"Love your neighbour as you love yourself,"* and then conduct the following experiment as objectively and honestly as possible.

Think for a few moments about how you see yourself, what you do for yourself, how you judge your failings, how you measure your accomplishments, how you trust your decisions and the degree to which you feel secure enough to move out of your comfort zone into areas of new experience. Make these observations part of a framework of awareness which questions the degree and strength of your self-love. Now think of someone who you genuinely love, both *totally* and *unconditionally*, then ask yourself some personal questions about your relationship with that person and think carefully about your responses. Some of those questions might be:

• What do I do when that person makes a mistake? What do I say to them? How do I judge them? How far do I go in my forgiveness of them? Do I search for an understanding as to why they erred? Do I condemn them or forgive them? Do I say to them, "I love you, not because of, or even in spite of your faults. I love you because my love for you is super-sighted and sees your very special qualities. My love for you is an unconditional gift." Do you do that with yourself when you make a mistake or do you bring out the hammer and nails and begin a second crucifixion? *Q: To what extent do you forgive yourself?*

• What do I do when that person I love believes they have a talent, skill or interest that they wish to pursue, like singing, writing or acting ? How do I encourage them? What do I do if they put obstacles in their own path? What if they express doubts as to the value of their interest? Would I ask to see their work, critiquing it gently and constructively, always encouraging them to go further? Would you do this for yourself? Or would you *automatically* put the needs of family, friends or your job before yourself? Have you ever wanted to play a musical instrument? As mentioned earlier, if you practised just thirty minutes a day for six months you could play almost any musical instrument with a relative degree of competence. If your friend wanted to, you would encourage them, so why not yourself? *Q: Do you have a talent, skill or interest that you wish to pursue? How have you pursued it? How have you dealt with any obstacles? How quickly did you give up your dream and why? How reasonable were the reasons you gave yourself for giving up?*

• What do I do for this other person as an expression of my love? How happy am I in that person's company? How often do I buy them a small gift or token of my affection? When you love someone, you indulge them once in a while by buying them a nice gift, you make an effort to be alone with them and you take pleasure and joy in their pleasure and joy. Do you do this with yourself? When did you last go on a short trip on your own? *Q: Do you express love for yourself? If so, how often and in what way? How comfortable are you in your own company for long periods?*

• In what way do I encourage this person I love to take chances? To experience new things? To have the confidence to embrace a new challenge? What do I say to them to encourage them to do so? *Q: How comfortable are you in moving out of your comfort zone? Why? How flexible and innovative are you in dealing with new situations? To what extent do you trust your judgement, resilience and strength in dealing with a new experience?*

• When the person I love feels pain or is grieving – how do I comfort them? Do I allow them to feel their pain and share it with them or do I tell them to pull themselves together and get on with living? In what ways would I help them get through their anguish? I am sure that you would be available to them in many ways. The big question again is, would you be available to yourself in the same way and with the same compassion or would you say to yourself, "Adults don't cry" or "Put up with it, it's part of life" or even worse, "It's partly your own fault?" *Q: How do you handle your own pain? Do you allow yourself to feel it? Do you see your experience of pain or grief as a weakness or a natural expression of your humanity?*

• Am I sensitive to the needs of the person I love? Do I search for those needs and try where possible to see that they are fulfilled? Do I acknowledge that they are an *intrinsic* and vitally important part of their identity and represent who they are? *Q: To what extent are you conscious of your own needs and of your obligation to fulfil them? Do you see those needs as part of the fabric of who you are or blemishes to it that are not needed?*

When you have honestly and objectively been through this process of thinking, ask yourself whether you are as loving to yourself as you are to that other person. In regard to the negative areas, you might begin the process of asking yourself, *"What is it in my personal Vision that prevents me from doing so?"*

If in any area of your Vision you find that you are *more* loving, generous and understanding to another, it is because at some time in the development of your self-esteem it became damaged or distorted.

The basis of practising self-love is to be as gentle, non-judgemental and above all as understanding with yourself as you would be to someone else you love unconditionally. The roots of self-development are too tangled to be effectively judged and it is a painful psychological truth that when you do judge yourself, you are often far harsher and frequently more cruel in that judgement than you should be.

Practising self-love involves the regular practice of positive self-esteem, an insistence on your right to be taken seriously, a balancing of your needs with those of others and an avoidance of voluntary inequality. For any relationship to be effective it must be based on a mutual acceptance of each other's value and not on the actions of a compulsive pleaser or a voluntary doormat.

You cannot genuinely love another unless you truly love yourself first. The first step is to love yourself in much the same way as you love someone else, and do for yourself what you do for them. The simple truth of the matter is that if you want to be loved by anyone, including yourself, you have to be lovable. To be lovable you must be loving, forgiving, understanding, merciful and often indulgent. Remember that in accordance with the principles of Vision Renaissance described earlier, even if you are not currently self-loving, as long as you act in accordance with the belief that you are, those attitudes you hold and the feelings you have will begin to lean in that direction. One of my favourite stories is a lovely folktale from Norway that illustrates the principle that if you act (or feel or think) in accordance with a desired reality, it will become real.

An ugly troll fell in love with a beautiful maiden who he saw wandering in the hills. To get her attention he donned a mask and dressed as a handsome prince. He quickly realized, however, that just looking the part was not enough, so he began to act like a prince who was worthy of a beautiful maiden. He was noble, gracious and generous to all, and it must have worked because she married him and for a while they lived together happily. But illusions must sometimes falter and one day she said to him, "I know you are wearing a mask, but you must know that I love you even without it. Take it off or I will leave you forever." Realizing that he had no choice he slowly removed it and underneath was — a handsome and noble prince.

The special mystery of the story, however, is the question, Was it the troll or the maiden who was transformed? In the Vedantic tradition of India, the principle is more simply stated: *"As a man acts, so does he become. As is man's desire so is his destiny."*

This was clearly demonstrated to me some years ago when a student spoke to me after a seminar asking how she could lift a depression without using medication. An attractive girl whose husband had left her after only a few months of marriage, she had put on a lot of weight due to overeating, and was smoking and drinking in excess. "I hate myself," was her sad reflection. I suggested that for the next thirty mornings and whenever she went into the bathroom, she should look intently at herself in the mirror, and when she was really in touch with her reflection, to embrace herself and *with as much genuine feeling as possible* pinch her cheek and say, "I love you." She was reluctant and embarrassed to do this at first, explaining that she certainly didn't feel self-loving. When I suggested that it was strange that although she was certainly willing to say "I love you" to another person, she was reluctant to do so in a private room to the most important person she should love. She relented, however, and did so. She advised me later that her depression had lifted, commenting, "You cannot go to work depressed, when, ten minutes before, you have told yourself with passion and with feeling that you were wonderful and loved." Maria's loving actions, which were artificially created at first, eventually created genuine thoughts and feelings and these happy feelings became the affirming feedback that reinforced the thoughts and made them authentic.

As you practise the various exercises in this chapter, ask yourself exactly how you express your love to those who are important to you and make a habit of doing the same things for yourself. See yourself as a very special person, knowing that if the emotions of love are not entirely present to begin with, your actions will begin to create their reality. But don't forget that in order for you to be loved by anyone, including yourself, you have to be lovable.

Let us now have a brief look at YOUR personal image of self. Please complete the following exercise as honestly and as objectively as possible. In other words, this is a test of how you see yourself, NOT how you *would* or *should* like to see yourself, or how your friends *may* think you see yourself:

A CHECK ON YOUR IMAGE OF SELF

Exercise #5

The following statements can each be rated with the words NEVER through to ALWAYS as indicated below. Make your choice and write in the space provided the number closest to the word you have chosen. Remember that your answer should reflect how you feel, not what you would like.

1 – Never	2 – Rarely	3 – Sometimes
4 – Quite frequently	5 – Almost always	6 – Always

(1) I am comfortable at social gatherings   _____

(2) People admire me   _____

(3) I enjoy attending to my personal needs   _____

(4) I see myself as a good-looking person   _____

(5) I see myself as a confident person   _____

(6) I see myself as a sharing person   _____

(7) I balance my life (rest, work, play)   _____

(8) I respect myself   _____

(9) I like my present situation   _____

(10) I am worthy of the gifts I have been given   _____

(11) I see myself as intellectually competent   _____

(12) I think that others value my opinions   _____

(13) When people hurt my feelings I tell them   _____

(14) I never compare my achievements to others   _____

(15) I am satisfied with my personal development   _____

(16) I enjoy meeting and talking with new people   _____

(17) I make a positive contribution to others   _____

(18) I enjoy my time alone   _____

(19) I see myself as attractive to the opposite sex _____

(20) I see myself as a loving person   _____

(21) I see myself as a successful person   _____

(22) I see myself as an independent free spirit   _____

(23) I see myself as being considerate to others   _____

(24) I look forward to getting up in the morning   _____

(25) I am happy with my present lifestyle   _____

(26) I am happy to be me rather than anyone else   _____

(27) I am a welcome addition to social gatherings   _____

(28) I am a valued friend   _____

(29) I can be relied upon   _____

(30) I see myself as dependable and responsible   _____

                                       Total =   _____

The maximum score that can be obtained in this exercise is 180.
Your self-image score can be broadly evaluated as follows:

Up to 45= Negative
Up to 75= Quite negative
Up to 105 = Positive and healthy
Up to 135 = Good
Up to 180 = Possibly unrealistic

Negative scores should not be feared, as they usually project a *realistically* negative self-image that can be improved by practising both S.A.F.E.R. and C.M.E.A. Very high scores, on the other hand, should be viewed cautiously, as they may be unrealistic and artificially created. The unfortunate "everybody likes and loves me" character may well have a confident and dynamic self-image but it may not be matched by the reality of a lonely life.

It is important for those with either negative or very positive scores to be very aware of feedback and to ask the questions, *"How do I know this image is true?"* and, *"Is this self-image justified by the feedback that I regularly receive?"* An honest evaluation of this will often provide the fertile ground in which a negative self-image can be improved and an unrealistic one made more realistic. One practical way to obtain and evaluate this feedback is to prepare an honest list of all the characteristics that you like about yourself, finding as many examples as you can, even if you feel that the list is too self-congratulatory. It could include (but should not be limited to) such traits as: loyalty, honesty, sincerity, courage, authenticity, charm, diplomacy, confidence, and thoughtfulness to others. When the list is complete, ask a couple of honest and objective friends and a couple of equally honest acquaintances to list the personal qualities that *they* most admire about you. A quick review of the completed lists may well prove very enlightening. Individuals with a low self-image and with few items on their list may find that the list completed by their acquaintances has far more positive qualities, and that these increase the closer the relationship. As mentioned earlier, a study of such simple feedback may well begin a dramatic change of self-image. On the other hand, individuals with a long list and with an apparently high self-image may find the reverse, that their acquaintances and friends do not confirm the list of their positive qualities.

Now complete the following exercise as further practice in applying the principles of Vision Renaissance.

Exercise # 6

LIST THREE QUALITIES that you would most like to have and which you do not have to the degree that you would like. For example:

Spontaneous
Loving
Open to change
Understanding
Adventurous
More carefree
Greater self-esteem

———————————————

———————————————

———————————————

The following is a sample list of attitude distortions that are part of the belief system of many people. Each of them, however, is irrational, illogical and life-diminishing. Think about each one carefully and the degree to which it may influence how you see yourself and the way you live your life.

COMMON ERRORS IN OUR BELIEF
SYSTEM ABOUT THE IMAGE OF SELF

1) I *MUST* be loved or approved by those who are significant to me *OR ELSE* I cannot love or approve myself.

2) I *MUST* be perfectly competent, adequate and successful in at least one area of my life *OR ELSE* I am not worth much.

3) I *MUST* please others and satisfy their expectations of me *OR ELSE* I am a failure.

4) I *MUST* always keep the peace in all my relations *OR ELSE* I will be failing in my duty.

5) I *MUST* always be in control of the situations in my life *OR ELSE* I will be in some form of danger.

6) *I MUST* avoid saying what I really think *OR ELSE* others may not like me.

7) I *MUST* keep quiet and not give my opinion *OR ELSE* I will appear pushy and inconsiderate.

8) I *MUST* keep telling others about my achievements or the important people I know *OR ELSE* they will not see my value.

9) *UNLESS* I satisfy others, I am a failure.

10) I *MUST* be loved and approved by people who know me *OR ELSE* I cannot love myself.

11) I *MUST* be my own harshest critic *OR ELSE* I will not improve.

12) I *MUST* avoid trying to do new things *OR ELSE* I might fail and look foolish.

13) If other people are angry with me, I usually think that it's *MY FAULT.*

14) I *MUST* not affirm, compliment or be too kind to others; *IF I DO,* they will feel superior to me and I will be vulnerable.

15) I *MUST* always be busy in some valuable venture *OR ELSE* I will be wasting my time.

16) I cannot love myself or express my needs *BECAUSE* I will be seen as arrogant and conceited.

17) I *MUST* dwell on my past failures *OR ELSE* I will not benefit from them.

18) I *MUST* always put the needs of others before mine *OR ELSE* I will be lacking in true goodness.

19) When others act in a way I do not like, I *MUST* avoid rather than understand them *OR ELSE* I'll waste my time.

Exercise #7

Using the previous nineteen statements as examples, please complete the following exercise:

Which of the above examples may be keeping you from attaining each of the three desirable qualities you listed at the beginning of the previous exercise? (several might apply). For instance, if you chose "more spontaneous and carefree", this would be seriously affected by statement #'s 1, 5, 12 and 16. A greater *understanding* of others by statement #'s 5, 14 and 19.

1 _____

_____

2 _____

_____

3 _____

_____

COUNTER-LOGIC

Now in your own words, devise and list below a counter-logic that directly challenges the lack of logic in each of the above. (Example: If for low self-esteem you chose: I *MUST be loved or approved by those who are significant to me OR ELSE I cannot love and approve myself* (#1 above), your counter-logic could be: *The only true failure is not to be open to growth.*)

1. _____

_____

2. _____

_____

3. _____

_____

Remember that the most important part of your belief system is the judgement that you make upon yourself. There is no value judgement more important, no factor more decisive in your psychological development and motivation than the estimate that you pass upon your own value. This influences every other perception that you have. It is only when you truly love, honour and respect yourself and believe in your unconditional right to be here enjoying the fruits of life that you are "free" from self-doubt and a primitive fight for survival. It is only then that you can truly unite with and love another on equal terms, not by a controlling demand that they be part of you, nor in a self-sacrificing submission which demands that you be part of them, but as an expression of your own self-love reaching out eagerly for a new beloved.

Irrespective of whether your self-image is correct or an illusion, it is projected to other people and they act upon it. By identifying any false beliefs regarding the way you see yourself and by using the methods of countering, modelling, expanding and affirming to change them you will create a healthier Vision of self and achieve a more loving union with those around you.

In the following chapter I will look at the second method of developing an authentic and unconditionally loving self-image. This is a highly effective but quite demanding process of proactive affirmation that requires a strong commitment to yourself and your growth, but *I can guarantee that if you practise it regularly, your life will change completely.*

On the next page let us look once again at the main points of this chapter.

SUMMARY OF CHAPTER SIX

1. There are four areas of your personal Vision: How you see yourself, others, the world of things (and values) and life itself. The most important of these is your Vision of self, because it is this that guides everything you do, experience, risk or feel.

2. This Vision is developed from the judgement that you make (self-esteem) on the collection of mentally held pictures that you hold of yourself (self-image). It is this judgement that directly influences every other aspect of your life.

3. A negative self-esteem can be changed by using the process of Vision Renaissance.

4. An essential aspect of self-esteem is a genuine, unconditional and regularly practised self-love. This can be defined as doing and feeling for oneself those things that you would do and feel for someone else who you genuinely and unconditionally loved.

5. Self-love is not to be confused with selfishness, which usually arises from self-contempt rather than self-love and which is on the opposite side of the personal growth spectrum.

6. Self-love can be encouraged and developed at any point in the self-development continuum even though *the newly conceived attitude is not yet believed*. Examples include: acting towards yourself in a loving manner (expanding), mentally affirming self-love in words and counter-logics (countering) and feeling loving about yourself (modelling). Each of these, when they are *regularly* practised, will reinforce the others and produce affirming feedback.

Chapter Seven

PRINCIPLES OF SELF-AFFIRMATION

"Who you are and who you will become is mainly a reflection of what the outside world thinks you are."
               Anonymous

"And since you know you cannot see yourself so well as by reflection, I, your glass, will modestly discover to yourself, that of yourself, which you yet not know of."
            William Shakespeare

"People are the only mirror we will ever see ourselves in."
            Lois McMaster Bujold

"In many cases people are what you make them. A scornful look turns a man of average intelligence into a complete fool. A contemptuous indifference turns into an enemy a woman who, well treated, might have been an angel."
            Andre Maurois

"We become what our environment tells us we are. We had better make sure it tells us the right things."
            Anonymous

"A friend's eye is a good mirror."
            Celtic proverb

As previously discussed, a positive and unconditionally loving image of self is the most important aspect of our personal Vision, but we were not born with it. Our self-image is created, developed and maintained by those around us who are encouraged by our actions to affirm who we are. It is based on an objective, freely given and exterior confirmation of our value and not on a subjective and needy search for approval.

In the story of Rapunzel, she was freed from her imagined limitations by the feedback from the prince, who told her that she was beautiful. Within this Grimm's fairy tale is an important aspect of human development, namely, that your image of self is essentially the product of the positive or negative feedback that you receive. How can you encourage your environment to freely give you the positive feedback that initially creates and then maintains a self-image that is healthy, fulfilling and life-enhancing?

Vision Renaissance suggests that others will affirm a healthy vision of self if you practise the following seven prerequisites of affirmation. Some of them are tough and require self-discipline, but I can guarantee that if you practise them regularly you will be amazed by the results.

THE SEVEN BUILDING BLOCKS OF AFFIRMATION

(1) Proclaim yourself
(2) Avoid self-promotion
(3) Practise unconditional self-love
(4) Challenge your fears and inhibitions
(5) Do not judge others
(6) Affirm those around you
(7) Commit yourself to the growth of others

Let us now look individually at each of these.

(1) PROCLAIM YOURSELF

What does this mean in practical terms? It means expressing all of your emotions, both negative and positive, in an honest and fearless manner. It means presenting to the world a faithful picture of who you are, what you think and what you feel. This is the core of a truly authentic self. It is only when you are able to express yourself in a genuine way that you develop the feeling, and from there, the reality, that the outside world knows *you*. It is only when people really know you that the reflection and feedback (affirmation) that you receive from them will verify and confirm your developing self-image.

Practise telling others what you really think about discussed issues. Express your thoughts and feelings fully and clearly whilst at the same time allowing the other person to tell you theirs. It is said that you can share almost anything with another person and not really be known by them. You can share a job, a partnership, a friendship, marriage, even sex and still be a total stranger to the other person involved, but it is only when you share your feelings, dreams, fears, hopes and pain, that your real identity becomes known. It is only then that the outside world can stand in front of you like Rapunzel's prince and say, "I see you, I understand you, I know you, and this is who you are." Only then can you begin a journey of authentic growth.

Recently at one of my seminars, a young lady suggested that she could not express herself in this way, as it would mean that some people would not like her. This may at times be true, as it is obviously impossible for everyone to like every aspect of everyone else, but this is better than pretending to be someone you are not. This is exhausting and because it is not true it is profoundly damaging to your personal growth.

The alternative to expressing *exactly* who you are is to make a judgement of the other person's needs, wants or admirations and to present yourself to them in a nice, neatly prepared package adjusted according to those needs. *The overriding problem in doing this is that irrespective of whether your judgement is correct or incorrect your personal growth will suffer.*

If your assessment of another's needs is *correct* and you express qualities that are not authentic in order to conform to them, you will carry the weight of that deception until you have to release both it and ultimately the friendship upon which it was dubiously based. At the same time, the affirming feedback will confirm an illusion. These twin deceptions eat into and weaken the development of an authentic self.

Conversely, if your assessment of another's needs is *incorrect*, you will have not only created feedback that confirms an illusion but you may have lost the opportunity for a genuine relationship with someone who needs or admires the qualities you have hidden. You would then have to implement what would appear to be a dramatic and maybe even manipulative personality change in order to redeem the relationship, if indeed it were possible to do so. Let us now look at a couple of examples:

Bill is a quiet and thoughtful young man who doesn't like to travel too much but who does like to read and play the guitar. He's a little shy and prefers to "take it easy" in the development of his relationships, not particularly enjoying superficial friendships. When his friendships do develop, however, they are deeply meaningful to him and he is loyal in maintaining them. Bill meets Anne at a party and is instantly attracted to her outgoing and vivacious personality. He speaks to her briefly about her job and interests and concludes *correctly* that she likes and admires extroverted and adventurous people who make friends easily. Bill, in his anxious desire to be approved and hoping to create a positive impression, begins to weave an illusion. He tells her that he loves to travel, constructing a few stories to prove it, embellishes his job significantly, and does not tell Anne that he reads a lot, as she does not appear to be much of a reader. Anne naturally gives him positive and encouraging feedback but this is based on an illusion that has to be maintained if the developing relationship is to continue. This illusion not only diminishes Bill's authentic self, but also reduces the opportunity for him to make friends with someone else who may have admired the qualities he has hidden.

Louise, on the other hand, is an assertive and ambitious business executive with a strong sense of ethics who believes that effective employees are those who are prepared to "rock the boat" a little, who express their opinions freely and honestly and who are prepared to defend them. Louise really doesn't like to "suck up" or to be overly subservient to the boss, as she genuinely believes that good leaders respect independent and forthright employees. Louise's new boss, Leonard, clearly indicates in his first few days that he admires and encourages independent employees and dislikes "yes men". Unfortunately

Louise doesn't believe him, thinking that he really prefers the opposite to this. Based on her *incorrect* assumption she adjusts her approach and presents herself as the type of employee that the new boss in fact dislikes. The feedback she then receives will reflect the boss's disdain and from that point on their relationship will be damaged by an ever-widening deception.

Another young woman once asked me whether she should tell her boss that she did not like him, believing that if she did so it would be to her disadvantage. The immediate and possibly surprising answer was that she should, because he almost definitely knew her feelings already. Most of us function at two levels of awareness: that of immediate and obvious observation, and at a deeper instinctive level that observes and interprets the subtleties of body language and vocal intonation. At this second level, where human intuition is often infallible, the boss probably realizes the truth but is unable to deal with it constructively. Receiving genuine opinions that are *appropriately expressed* will allow him to do so.

In expressing your feelings openly in this way, it is important that they be expressed for the right motive. If you are merely "getting it off your chest", by dumping your problems onto somebody else's lap, people will only feel pity for you or at worst will feel manipulated. A genuine expression of your feelings is a gift based on trust. In reality you are saying, *"In sharing my feelings with you, I am choosing to trust you with who I really am, it is the most important possession that I have and it is my unconditional gift to you."* In doing so it becomes a positive affirmation of who they are as well as you.

There is, however, a fundamentally important way of expressing your feelings without creating a defensive response, and that is to *accept and own your emotions and to express that ownership by making "I" statements instead of "you" statements.* No one else can create painful or negative feelings in you. They can certainly stimulate or inflame them but *they cannot create them.* Telling someone by words or actions that they have done so is not true and will almost always cause them to become defensive. Why is this? Compare the following two fairly typical statements:

"You really make me angry when you ignore me at parties and socialize with other people."

"You really make me mad when you arrive late every time we have a date."

The other person will usually react with defensive anger when you express yourself in this manner because *subconsciously* they know that you are attacking them with two very destructive lies.

Lie #1 implies that the other person can physically create your anger. This is obviously untrue.

Lie #2, is even more offensive as it implies that they purposely do so, and possibly with malicious intent. Only seriously deranged individuals *purposely* hurt others for no reason. People may stimulate angry feelings in others *by default* but not from intentional malice.

Compare the above two statements with the following, which express the same intent but which accept ownership of the emotions expressed.

"When you socialize too much with other people at parties instead of with me, I get angry, and upset. I don't want to get angry so would you please try not to do it."

"When you arrive late, I really get uptight. Can you try to arrive earlier? I'm sure that I will enjoy our time together so much more if you do."

Try this experiment: Choose two equally significant things that a friend does that annoy you. Take the first of these, and tell them that they make you very angry when they do it. Respond as you would normally do to their response and note the results.

A little later mention the other item, but in the second way mentioned above. Again, note both their and your *usual* response. Then ask yourself which approach was most likely to achieve your goals.

"You" statements create passion, anger and heat. "I" statements create understanding.

There is an additional and very important factor that must also be considered and that is, if you don't honestly *express* your emotions externally, you will either *act* them out on your loved ones or friends or you will internalize them and this will affect your health. Emotions will be expressed one way or the other and will not be eliminated just by being ignored or repressed. There is a lot of wisdom in the old suggestion, *"Don't bottle it up inside."* If you do, it will eventually be to the detriment of those around you or it will internally fester where it will manifest itself in self-destructive acts (smoking, drinking, overwork, overeating) or disease (cancer, hypertension and heart disease), but it will not go away of its own accord. You cannot escape an unexpressed emotion.

Being yourself and expressing as honestly as possible who you are, what you want and how you feel is ultimately far less exhausting and creates far less turmoil than wearing a mask. When you present to the world who you really are, with all your human limitations, frailties and fears on the one hand and your accomplishments, talents, needs, emotions and opinions on the other, it is important to realize that you are not presenting *the reality* or *the truth* but you are presenting *your reality* and *your truth.* This is reflected back from the world around you and begins the process of initially creating, then reinforcing and finally maintaining a truly authentic self. In doing so it is imperative that neither culture, environment, family nor social expectations be allowed to impose their own unreal expectations of what *they* think you should be, even when this is done under the auspices of love, respect and protection.

(2) AVOID SELF-PROMOTION

The second of the seven building blocks of self-affirmation concerns the tendency that many people have of affirming themselves by self-promotion as an alternative to receiving it from others. It is important that you avoid all attempts at self-promotion, such as bragging, gamesmanship, status symbols, petty attempts at one-upmanship and boasting about who or what you know in an attempt to impress others. This is not genuine self-expression; rather it is usually either a mean-spirited attempt to prove yourself at the expense of others or a manipulative presentation of a package of skills, talents and accomplishments based on your perception of their needs.

True affirmation is based on an objective and exterior confirmation of your personal value and not on a subjective and needy search for approval. If, by your words and actions, you constantly seek approval, respect, or admiration, the gentlest and most loving response will be pity but most of the time you will be resented.

(3) PRACTISE UNCONDITIONAL SELF-LOVE

The importance of becoming unconditionally self-loving has been discussed in much greater detail in previous chapters. It is, however, of vital importance to emphasize once again that the way others determine who you are and how they should act towards you is based solely on the information that you present to them about yourself. If you act as if you have value, others will act as if you are valuable. If you act as if you care for and love who you are, others will begin to care for and love those self-loving qualities you project.

Conversely if you act as if you are insignificant and unworthy of consideration, the treatment you receive from others will reflect your insignificance and lack of value. We have discussed earlier the importance of authenticity and it is imperative that the image you project be honestly felt and sincerely constructed and not an illusion.

(4) CHALLENGE YOUR FEARS AND INHIBITIONS

The fourth of the seven factors involved in a framework for self-affirmation is to be aware of and to constantly challenge your fears and inhibitions. It is only then that others will fully relate to you in a positive, secure manner and will affirm that in some way you enrich their lives. I think that we all know individuals who are constantly *"playing it safe"*. Individuals who have to *"know the territory"* before they move out of their comfort zone and make a decision, and whose security and identity are based on the known and familiar. Unfortunately we can never really relate positively to them, as deep down they offer us very little. Their lack of adventure and narrowness of vision do not enrich us. At best, we will feel sorry for them, but our pity will only confirm their own insecurity. It is a poignant fact of life that we are mainly guided by self-interest and are attracted to others because in some way their qualities enrich our life, and by our actions to them we confirm those qualities.

Fear, or more specifically, fear of fear, and the need to conform that it creates are crippling emotions and we must strive to overcome them. Paradoxically, however, they are important in that we are biologically programmed to fear new situations and to conform to the old in order to survive. It is important to realize, however, that fear and the need to conform are the same emotions that tend to prevent our growth as authentic individuals and it is this conflict which is often at the heart of the human dilemma.

Effective personal development usually demands the recognition of, and participation in, those experiences that involve a lessening of security. For many people this is difficult and it is easier to avoid, but it is possible to develop beliefs that encourage the process. These include:

• *Irrespective of your fear, take "baby steps" to overcome it.*

It is not easy to totally overcome a fear by suddenly confronting it in its totality. The secret is to attack it slowly and in small manageable steps, knowing that at each step retreat to security is possible. It is only then that the subconscious mind can evaluate the feedback in terms of your survival and comfort level.

• *Ask yourself, what is the worst that can happen, and how bad that would be?*

Ultimately, the reason you are afraid is that you feel something bad is going to happen to you. Your imagination generally exaggerates those bad things in order to prevent you moving from a comfortable security. Counter this by asking, *What is the worst thing that could reasonably happen? What is the second or third worst thing? How probable is this? What will happen to me if the worst thing does occur, and can I survive if it does?* Remember that even if the worst thing *does* happen, you will at least have the comfort of knowing that you tried, survived, were not afraid and gained a new experience.

• *Am I so different from others who do what I am afraid to do? If not, what is it in ME that is making ME afraid?*

Observing the qualities of similar people who do what you are afraid to do compels you to look at yourself and your own motivation a little more closely. What is it in your perception of life and your interpretation of the specific risks involved that makes you different from other people who are not afraid?

• *How much of my fear is reasonable and how much is irrational?*

Shakespeare wrote, *"Our thoughts are traitors and make you lose the good you oft might win by fear of the attempt!"* It is an axiom of psychology that, *"When reason and emotion are in conflict, emotion will generally win."* It is therefore imperative in conquering fear, that you ask if your fear is reasonable. If it is not, it is neurotically based. Fear that a plane may crash is reasonable because planes do crash. A paralysing fear that avoids flying, on the basis that *your* plane will *probably* crash, is not.

• *How much of the "irrational" part of my fear is based on incorrect messages received as a child?*

As discussed earlier, your Vision of life is composed of countless beliefs that constantly evaluate your personal reality. One of these concerns new experience. Is that evaluation appropriate to your well-being? Is fear an emotion that should *always* be avoided, or are there occasions when it should be embraced for the sake of experience? How do you identify these occasions? Is the world *inherently* dangerous? Think about the likely effect of the following beliefs compared with their alternative counter-logic.

I must be capable and competent in most things that I attempt, otherwise I will be in great danger.

Obviously you cannot be competent in something until you try it. An appropriate counter-logic might well be:

I will be secure if I confront new experiences and learn the skills needed to deal with them before, during and after the experience.

People are not trustworthy and have to be watched all the time OR ELSE they will take advantage of, use or otherwise manipulate me.

Think what this will do to your personal relationships. An appropriate counter-logic might well be:

Other people are just like me and need love, kindness and support. I will be secure with them if I treat them accordingly.

The world "out there" is a very dangerous place, and you have to avoid getting involved with it as much as possible.

This one will really limit your sense of adventure and your enjoyment of life. The following is much more effective.

The world out there is full of exciting and wonderful possibilities. I will be secure and happy if I embrace these opportunities while exercising reasonable caution.

And finally:

Be Careful!!!!!!!!!!!!!

This caution if expressed by parents *every* time a child leaves home, climbs a tree or goes for a swim, is particularly damaging to a child's growth. Yes, reasonable caution is imperative and it is a parent's responsibility to suggest that caution be exercised and why, but to constantly imply that the world outside the front door (comfort zone) is overly dangerous is toxic to an individual's ability to grow. Authentic individuals recognize the subject of their fear and why they are afraid of it, but do not *automatically* feel the need to escape from it. They recognize the need for new challenge and experience as the main pathway to growth and embrace those new challenges with passion while accepting the fear that may accompany them.

(5) DO NOT JUDGE OTHERS

It is said that when you judge others your judgement will usually be wrong. Of greater importance is that the emotions and actions created by that erroneous judgement will be inappropriate. Each person with whom you interact is a highly complex product of their biological makeup, their background and their experiences. For you to make an instant judgement is to imply that you have x-ray vision and can see instantly through that complexity. Until you realize this, especially in regard to those with whom you have a "difficult" relationship, you can never even begin the process of communication. If you are in doubt as to a person's motivation, ask them about it, but be vigilant and cautious before acting upon your own unproven judgement.

You will remember the story told earlier of the young counsellor who commented a little harshly and judgementally on a young woman's negative attitude. He was firmly told to exercise great caution in making a judgement as to what was behind it. *"Did you ever have a toothache?"* effectively expressed our obligation to look below the surface of a person's actions and not to make hasty judgements.

The tendency to make rash judgements about the motivation of others often extends to the judgement you make about your own. Try this small experiment. Think of someone you dislike and with whom you work or have worked. Write down the major reasons that you think motivate your disdain. Now, and as realistically as possible, imagine the following scenario. You are standing at the coffee shop waiting to be served and this person is waiting behind you. At an appropriate moment they look at you, smile, wish you good morning and say, *"You know something, we've worked together for several years and I've always had a tremendous respect for your efficiency and professionalism, it's always bothered me that we don't get along. I really wish that we did. I just thought I'd like to tell you that."* At that moment, most of your dislike would probably vanish, but your "reasons" are still there and still exist.

This is obviously a slightly contrived example, but it does serve to illustrate that in most cases the *real* reason for your dislike is the belief that the other person does not like, value or respect you, and not the ones that you previously gave.

When you correctly identify the true cause of a problem, you are often in a much stronger position to solve it.

(6) AFFIRM OTHERS

Inherent in the process of exterior affirmation is a mutual obligation to esteem and affirm others. We need people as friends, helpers and shoulders to cry on in order to survive. How we obtain and keep them is one of the main keys to our survival and growth.

You often see people who sail through their relationships with a gentle ease, who are popular, who have a network of helpers and whose lives are made easy by the comforting touch of those around them. You can say they have charisma, personality, charm or style, but it is difficult to define the special qualities that make their lives so easy. One truth that they have all discovered is that you cannot really afford to have one enemy, and that survival lies in changing those who dislike you into being indifferent to you, those who are indifferent to you into becoming your friends, and those who are your friends into greater friends.

How do you do this and at the same time keep your own personal integrity? The answer is really quite simple. You develop the art of sincerely building *their* self-esteem by searching for their positive qualities and letting them know that you have found them.

The art of affirming others is discussed in much greater detail in Chapter Eight, but how wonderful life would be if we all took the time to make others feel good about themselves. Try it, if only for a few days; your life may never be the same.

(7) COMMIT YOURSELF TO THE GROWTH OF OTHERS

The closest form of communication that you can have with another is that of unconditional love which manifests itself as a commitment to the growth of the beloved. The great spiritual disciplines throughout history have been united in their belief that unconditional love is the pathway along which the human spirit passes from selfishness to selfhood, from solitude to kinship, and from ignorance to understanding. The love they refer to is not that of passion, emotion or the possessive need that often masquerades as love, but a quality that transcends an individual's needs and sublimates them to the growth of another. When expressed, this unconditional love is usually given to an individual, or to a god in the form of an individual, (as with most religions) or to an idea, a country or a tradition.

As mentioned earlier, it is sometimes said that true love is blind and because of this people do not see the faults of those they love. This is not true; true love is actually "super-sighted", as it sees through the veneer of self-protection to the beautiful person beneath, affirms that beauty and is then committed to the growth, development and happiness of the beloved.

It may seem that the needs of self-interest often conflict with a loving commitment to another's growth. These are not mutually exclusive but are complementary to each other.

We all have *ever-increasing* survival needs, which start with the immediate basics of food and shelter. Having satisfied these we are then motivated by increasingly more complex ones such as long-term security, deepening companionship, community acceptance, recognition of personal value and finally an unfettered development of our unique potential as human beings. The fulfilment of each of these does not lessen the urge to grow but actually makes it more insistent. In many ways dissatisfaction can be seen as a sign of mental health rather than the reverse. At each stage, the drive forward is progressively more refined and outer-directed, embracing as it does a greater integration of one's own needs, then a union of those needs with those of a partner, one's family, community, mankind and finally with life itself.

The starting point is explicit self-interest, but as we will see later, genuine self-interest can only be maintained, protected and enhanced by integration with our outer world. These wider psychological demands which compel us to make a commitment to the needs of others are logical extensions of our physical ones and both stem from the same source, namely personal survival.

Your ability to put into effect these seven prerequisites for affirmation is directly affected by your Vision and any limitations within it that prevent you from doing so. The following exercise will help to isolate those limitations. When you have completed it, use the S.A.F.E.R. and C.M.E.A. methods to change them. Please try to answer the following eleven questions. It may help if you check your answers with a friend because although you may think that you express your feelings freely (#4), challenge your fears readily (#10), and that you do not judge others too harshly (#3), those around you might not agree. Their opinions will balance your own.

Exercise #8

PREREQUISITES FOR SELF-AFFIRMATION

1. Avoid self-promotion (boasting, bragging, name-dropping, etc). *Which of these are you most tempted to practise?*

_____

_____

Why? _____

_____

2. Practise unconditional self-love. *In what circumstances do you tend to be blinded to your good qualities?*

_____

_____

Why? _____

_____

3. Do not judge others or make assumptions about their emotions or motivation. *With what type of person or in what circumstance do you feel most inclined to make judgements or assumptions?*

_____

_____

Why? _____

_____

4. Express all your emotions freely and fully – both negative and positive. *Which emotion(s) do you feel least free to experience or express?*

_____

_____

Why? _____

_____

5. Demand respect. *When and with whom do you find it hardest to demand respect for your person and your rights?*

_____

_____

Why? _____

6. Proclaim your "self." *In what circumstances do you find it most difficult to be honest and open about what you think, feel and need?*

_____

_____

Why? _____

_____

7. Be gentle with yourself. *What perceived weakness in you results in the most severe self-criticism?*

_____

_____

Why? _____

_____

8. Affirm others and commit yourself to their growth. *With what person or type of person do you find it most difficult to be understanding and loving?*

_____

_____

Why? _____

_____

9. Affirm others, look for what is good in them and express your appreciation and praise. *What good qualities in others do you find it most difficult to accept, appreciate or praise and when does this happen?*

_____

_____

Why? _____

_____

10. Challenge your fears and inhibitions. *By what fear or inhibition do you feel most limited?*

_____

_____

Why? _____

_____

11. Commit yourself to the growth of others. *What individuals within your immediate caring community do you feel least able to encourage and motivate?*

_____

_____

Why? _____

_____

Although some of these are tough, regular practice of the seven building blocks of self-affirmation will provide the fertile environment in which a fully authentic and genuine identity can be affirmed and developed.

In this chapter we have discussed bridging the gulf between the beliefs that you hold about yourself and their positive development by outside affirmation. We will now turn to the second growth area of your Vision, that of other people. In particular the question: What is a healthy Vision of others?

SUMMARY OF CHAPTER SEVEN

1. Who you are and who you become is primarily a result of the feedback (affirmations) that you receive from the outside world. This can be positive or negative.

2. This feedback is based on how you present yourself to the outside world.

3. By regular practice of the seven building blocks of affirmation you will encourage the outside world to affirm a positive and life-enhancing identity.

   - *Express your emotions*
   - *Avoid self-promotion*
   - *Practise unconditional self-love*
   - *Challenge your fears and inhibitions*
   - *Do not make assumptions about the thoughts, feelings or motivation of others*
   - *Affirm the value of others*
   - *Commit yourself to the growth of those around you*

Chapter Eight

LIVING WITH OTHERS

"We make our friends, we make our enemies, but God makes our next-door neighbour. That is why the old religions and the old scriptural language showed so sharp a wisdom when they spoke, not of one's duty toward humanity, but of one's duty to one's neighbour. Duty towards humanity may take the form of choice, which is pleasurable, personal or necessary. But we have to love our neighbours because they are there – a much more alarming reason for a much more serious operation. They are the actual sample of humanity which is given to us – precisely because they may be anybody, they are everybody."

G.K.Chesterton

"If our brothers are oppressed, we are oppressed. If they hunger, we hunger. If their freedom is taken away, ours is not secure."   *Stephen V. Beet*

"A hundred times a day I remind myself that my inner and outer life depend on the labour of others, living and dead, and that I must exert myself in order to give in the same measure as I have received and am receiving."

Albert Einstein

"It is an inexorable law that one cannot deny another's humanity without diminishing one's own."   *James Baldwin*

"There is more power in the open hand than in the closed fist."

Herbert M.Casson

"Beginning today and just for one week, treat everyone you meet as if they were going to die by midnight. Extend to them all the care, kindness and understanding you can muster. Your life will never be the same."

Og Mandino

"Believe me every man has his own secret sorrow which the world knows not; and oftentimes we call a man cold when he is only sad."
                                                    Henry Wadsworth Longfellow

"A habit for all of you to develop is to look for something to appreciate in everyone you meet. We can all be generous with appreciation and praise because everyone is grateful for it and it improves every human relationship. It brings courage to those who are sorely challenged, renewed strength to the weak and endurance to those who are tired. So give appreciation sincerely and generously whenever you can. You will never regret it."   Carl Holmes

Aristotle wrote, *"Self-sufficiency is among the greatest of felicities."* As far as it goes, Aristotle was correct. However, to be able to enjoy your own company exclusively, and to provide for your own needs completely, is an ideal to which many people aspire but which very few achieve. In reality, you are dependent upon, and interdependent with, all those around you. No one can live as a hermit or a monk and believe for one moment that they are *totally* independent of others. The fact of the matter is that *you need other people in order to survive and your commitment to that need is the key to your survival.* This is a biological, sociological and emotional fact of your existence. It is vital that you understand and develop an effective way of relating with others in order to fill this need.

From the moment we are born and leave the unity, security and comfort of our mother's womb, it seems that we never get over the anguish of separation and the need to overcome it. *It is this feeling of separateness that is the source of much of our anxiety and it is the need to overcome it that is our main motivator.*

There are three paths that this quest for union may take. The mature individual, who from birth is gradually encouraged and permitted to accept the reality of separateness, pursues it by learning how to extend and fuse their own reality with that of others. In its finest expression, this manifests as love, commitment and creativity. Conversely, immature individuals who do not accept it, pursue the quest for unity by either becoming part of another by a *needy dependence* or by making others part of them by *control or manipulation*. All three paths, namely *integration, dependence* or *control*, contribute to the development of one's self-image and self-esteem. The first path, of integration however, leads to freedom and growth, while the latter ones of dependence and control lead to decay and neurosis and a failure to achieve *any* form of unity, to madness.

Before I discuss the imperative need that all of us have for others, please refer once more to the statement made earlier in this chapter: *"You need other people in order to survive and your commitment to that need is the key to your survival."* Do not make the common error that this commitment to others is primarily for their benefit or to fulfil an ethical obligation. It is for your own personal benefit and survival. *To maintain otherwise is to deny the very fact of your existence.* Let us look for a moment at the specifics of why you need others.

In their social environment, many people like to believe that they do not need others and that this is an expression of their strength. Although most of us are usually prepared to admit that we enjoy others and that they contribute to our well being, *needing* them is often seen as a weakness. In many ways this feeling is understandable, as the less dependent we are upon others, the less we feel at risk. The uncomfortable truth is that at no time in our social development as individuals, groups and as a species have we ever been totally free of the need for others. None of us are born with all the talents needed for survival. Indeed many survival talents cannot coexist in the same person. In primitive societies people needed others to help protect them from wild animals, to join in projects that needed varying skills, to protect their families and possessions from the predatory instincts of other groups and to merge the skills of their group with those of others to enhance their security.

In the primitive societies of Anglo-Saxon England for example, it was the gradual merging of the farming Anglos, who lacked the fighting skills to defend their farms, with the fearsome Saxon warriors, who lacked farming skills, which created the Anglo-Saxon cultural tradition. In more advanced societies like ours, those skills have become even more specialized and the need for interdependence is even greater than it has ever been. We all need doctors to heal us, builders to house us, farmers to feed us and warriors to defend us. Within each of these groups there are many specializations. Warriors have become soldiers, policemen, firemen and ambulance drivers; farmers have become bakers, cooks and dairymen; builders have become plumbers, electricians and painters and doctors have become nurses, surgeons and social workers, each providing the multitude of skills that are counted upon for survival.

But it is not only your social needs that others fulfil. Psychologically, your growth and emerging identity are *directly* dependent upon feedback from the people around you, their *positive* or *negative* reflection of your value being what ultimately develops and maintains your identity.

It is a basic fact that our life is shaped by those who love us, *and refuse to love us* and as John Powell so wisely suggested, *"Human beings, like plants, grow in the soil of acceptance, not in the atmosphere of rejection."* Our *emotional* needs also demand an ever-increasing union with the world around us and the amazing thing about sharing ourselves in this manner is that it increases our joy and reduces our pain. Erich Fromm describes this quest for union in his book, *The Art of Loving.* He suggests that the true meaning behind the biblical symbolism of Adam and Eve has been obscured by prudery. The shame of Adam and Eve was not in their nakedness, but in the realization that they were separate and had not learned how to love in order to redeem their union. As mentioned earlier, it is the pain of unresolved separation that is the source of much of our anxiety and the quest for its resolution that is the motive for creative and spiritual growth.

As pointed out in the previous chapter, it is a simple truth that if you want to be loved, you have to be lovable. To be lovable you must be loving, forgiving, understanding, merciful and often indulgent.

I have said earlier that your relationship with others is essentially self-serving. To people brought up in the tradition that it is better to serve others, this is a difficult premise to accept and to act upon, but your authentic development demands that you do both. It becomes more acceptable when developing individuals slowly begin to realize that the *apparent* conflict between the needs of others and of themselves is an illusion.

What then is an optimum way of dealing with others? The prerequisite, of course, as previously mentioned, is to have an unconditionally loving image of self.

If we are afraid of others, unsure of them or even hate them, it is almost always because we are unsure of our own strength, security and value. If we are unable to give these to another or if we do not possess them, we will inevitably try to take them away from those around us.

The first step is to realize that almost everyone you meet is similar to you in all those areas that are really important. Many people do not like to feel or admit this, believing that characteristics that divide are more significant than those that unite. Other people will intimidate you until you recognize this basic connection and the almost *universal* need for love, tolerance, acceptance and understanding. When we do not give this to others, and even worse, when we actively withdraw it, we are creating in others the anguish of separation and the need for self-protection. This will then be reflected back to us as non-acceptance of our value. When you truly recognize and understand this similarity with others, the need for love and acceptance that it includes and the reactions that follow when they are not forthcoming, you will also appreciate the vital fact that *you cannot afford one enemy.*

The first step therefore in dealing effectively with others is to realize the similarity of our mutual needs. The second step as briefly indicated in the previous chapter is to use that awareness to transform those that despise you into being indifferent to you, those that are indifferent to you into your friends and those who are your friends into even greater friends. How do you do this?

Let us profile once again a type of person that many of us know and admire. These individuals can be of either gender, any age, come from any social group and we can meet them anywhere. One thing they have in common however is an uncanny ability to get along with people and in so doing they float through life with an envied ease and calm. In the workplace, for example, they have the ear of management and are therefore respected by their subordinates because they listen, interact with them and can make their opinions known in the right areas. Management equally respects them because they have a feel for the issues and concerns of the staff and have a sensitive well-tuned ear to the dynamics of the organization. They are rarely subject to, or the victims of, the vagaries of office politics or gossip, and although their opinions are not always universally approved they are always listened to and respected. These individuals believe intuitively that success depends primarily on the well-being of others while most other individuals believe that their success depends primarily on their own. By acting in this way these individuals wield a subtle and almost magical influence on their immediate environment, an influence that cannot be readily identified with charm, power or appearance. They are in fact contemporary masters of four very special and almost magical arts that I will describe in the remaining part of this chapter. These are:

The Art of Pleasing
The Art of Effective Communication
The Art of Dealing with Conflict
The Art of Grace

THE ART OF PLEASING

It is easier and more pleasurable to please people than it is to offend them, and your life is far more comfortable and smooth when those around you enjoy you. The key to relating effectively with others lies in pleasing them. This is not a difficult art and does not require years of university education to learn. Neither does it imply a servile, self-denying flattery, but it does involve a genuine and cultivated appreciation of the individual worth of others and a genuine search for and *expression* of what is good and unique in them. Lord Chesterfield, one of England's great writers on practical human affairs, wrote in *Letters to His Son*, "Make a man like himself and he will like you in return", and these words are as valid now as they were two hundred years ago when they were written. Do everything *genuine* that you can to improve and develop the self-esteem of your fellow man. Most individuals have within them gems of true value. Find those redeeming features, tell them that you have done so and you will make them a staunch friend and an invincible ally. They will see that you have penetrated their veneer of self-protection and have seen the real person beneath. Genuine compliments on a person's style, wit, intelligence, looks or character, a child's small achievement or just a friendly good morning are the keys to pleasing, and what powerful keys they are. An obvious extension of pleasing, of course, is that you not intentionally displease, wound the vanity of another or make them look small, either by accident or intention, for they will never forgive you.

The master key to human nature is vanity. Look sincerely and genuinely for what is good in others, let them know what it is and you will have found the key to their friendship and their heart but your attempts must be genuine and sincere. Human instinct is almost infallible in this area. If you are merely trying to hook people in by insincere compliments, they may go along with the charade, but deep down they will know that you are lying and will despise you. If you cannot do this for any reason – smile. A smile is the most powerful tool of esteem that you have. *You* may smile because you feel good, but the receiver will always interpret your smile as, *"There is something about me that they like."* Affirm others by making appreciative comments,

"That was really kind of you," "How nice of you to ---," "Thank you so much for ---," and evaluative ones *"Well done," "You did well when you ---," "You are really good at ---"* and as mentioned below in communication techniques, do not forget that often it is not *what* you say but *how* you say it that matters.

Remember also that it is not only the words you use and how you use them that please, but also how you look. Appearances do count. A pleasing appearance, a well-tailored outfit and a confident self-assured manner will always be a strong initial recommendation. A ready smile, a genuine air of good will and a positive, happy disposition will always endear people to you. *Please people's eyes and you will please their mind. Please their mind and you will please their heart. Please their heart and they will be yours forever.* Practise the art of pleasing and your life will change.

THE ART OF EFFECTIVE COMMUNICATION

In addition to practising the art of pleasing, it is imperative that you also practise the art of effective communication. Why is the art of communication such a vital skill? The achievement of your personal needs is dependent upon the degree to which you can manipulate the world around you to fulfil them. This is achieved by your capacity to communicate.

Effective communication with the people around you is a vital factor in creating an authentic self. It is also the key to success in work and in all social interactions. You need effective communication skills and strategies to share ideas and experiences, to find out about things that interest you, to explain to people who you are and what you want and to express your feelings and insights. Effective communication is the way you bridge the gap between the reality of your inner self and that of the outside world and fuse them together into a functioning whole. The alternative is a separate, conflicting and often painful divide. If you communicate effectively with the people around you, you will begin to proactively shape your world as you wish it to be. If you do not, you will be shaped by the world as it is and usually to your disadvantage. In order to develop this powerful tool in your life, let us first understand what communication is and why it is vitally important.

Effective communication involves four components, and if any of these are missing, you are not communicating. These components are:

1) Initial transmission of information
2) Receipt of information
3) Receiver's understanding of sender's message
4) Acknowledgement of understanding to sender

On the surface these would appear to be both obvious and simple but a closer look will show that they are seldom fully practised. Let us look at each of them in greater detail.

1) Initial transmission of information

There is a tendency in close relationships to feel that the "other side" should have magical powers of insight and should know what you think and feel. You feel that they should be extra sensitive to your "vibes", subtle hints and the nuances of your body language. It would be nice if this were the case. Most people, however, are too involved with their own feelings and problems to be overly sensitive to yours. If you want to transmit information, do so *intentionally and clearly* and not by hints, or, as happens in some cases, in an oblique manner in order to manipulate.

2) Receipt of information

It is not sufficient to merely transmit information. It is also vitally important to ensure that it is received. A husband or wife who "turns off" their spouse by constant nagging or complaining, a speaker or teacher who is boring or a communicator who lacks the ability to grasp their audience's attention may well be transmitting information but it is will not being effectively received.

3) Understanding by the receiver of the sender's message

The purpose of communicating is to have people understand the information that is being sent. *Are you being too technical or complicated? Are you speaking at the intellectual, social and cultural level of your audience? Are you trying to be elitist? Are you trying to impress or inform?* These are questions the effective communicator should regularly ask of themselves. Cultural differences can be far more profound than you suspect. Members of some cultures will react with total embarrassment and even shame at being told quite gently that they have annoyed you; others will not react at all until your irritation is expressed far more forcibly. A complex concept can be explained in a few words to someone educated in it, but someone else may need a much more detailed, graphic and yet simpler explanation. In other words, how are *you* transmitting *your* message?

4) Acknowledgment

How can you *know* that *your* message has been understood so that you can progress further? Quite simply, you ask, you clarify, you watch for appropriate body language, and above all, you listen. Effective listening is the most powerful tool in the arsenal of human communication. When you listen effectively to other people speaking you are increasing their self-esteem by valuing what they are saying, confirming that their message has been received and understood, acknowledging their communicative capacity and encouraging their desire to communicate. As Sydney Smith wittily put it, *"The ability to speak several languages is a valuable asset but to be able to hold your tongue in one is priceless."*

The major tools at your disposal in effectively using the above four factors of communication are: (a) the way you speak,

(b) the words you use, (c) the body language you adopt, and (d) an awareness of the effect the first three tools are having on the person or group to whom you are speaking. Very often it is not *what* you say that matters but what the words *imply* and the *feelings* that they and your body language generate. Let us look briefly at the major considerations that should occur to you when speaking and using body language.

– Think about your purpose in communicating and what you are trying to achieve by your words and actions. *What do you want to achieve and will your words and body language achieve it?*

– Think about the words that you use and how you use them. Only 35 to 45 percent of meaning rests in the words that are used. The rest is determined by how they are used, your body language when you do so and the pitch, tone, emphasis and intonation of your voice. Your words do *not* create your listener's actions; your words evoke the emotions that then power those actions. *How do you speak? What is your body language saying? Are your words and body language congruent? What emotions are your words going to evoke in your listener? Are they accurate reflections of what you want to say?*

– Think of your audience. What do they want, need or expect from *your* communication in order to act in accordance with *your* wishes? *Will your audience understand the words that you are using and your reason for using them?*

Here are some ways that you can use your words, your awareness and your body language to improve your communication skills.

• Recognize the need to communicate.

• Try to see every situation from the other side.

- Get the listener's attention. (How? Motivate, interest or entertain).

- Do not assume that you know the listener's thoughts, feelings or motivation. If in doubt, ask.

- Know what you want to say before you start talking.

- Be brief, clear and coherent.

- Know what interests the listener.

- Be interested in the world around you.

- Like people.

- Ask open-ended questions. (These are questions that cannot be answered with a "yes" or "no" and which usually begin with how, why, when, who, what, where or tell me about etc).

- Maintain congruent body language. (For example, don't say, "I'm really interested in what you have to say," and then look out of the window)

- Listen, observe and clarify.

- Know how to end a conversation.

- Strive to establish personal relationships.

- Speak at your audience's social and cultural level.

The following amusing story will serve to illustrate *your* vital importance in the communication spectrum:

"An elderly man went to his doctor complaining that his wife had a communication problem in that whenever he spoke she ignored him. The doctor wisely suggested that before they both come in for a discussion, the old fellow should find out if his wife was deaf. In accordance with the doctor's instruction and when she was next cooking dinner he stood a little way behind her and asked what was for dinner. He was ignored. Stepping closer, he repeated the question twice more and was again ignored each time. Standing right behind her now, he loudly asked once again. At last she turned and in a loud voice exclaimed, " for the fourth time you deaf ole coot, it's chicken."

Effective communication is a loop of continuous cause and effect with you, the communicator, acting as both. Your boss, co-worker or employee does not have a communication problem. *If one exists, you should admit to yourself that you are part of the problem and the first person to look to for a solution.*

THE ART OF SOLVING CONFLICT

Earlier in this chapter I suggested that an optimum relationship with others involves the development of four interlocking personality skills: pleasing, communicating, dealing with conflict and grace. No matter how effective you are in dealing with others, there will always be times when you will be either in direct conflict with others or be part of a conflicting situation that involves them. Dealing effectively with other people involves being able to avoid, eliminate or diminish that conflict. In order to do this you have to recognize what conflict is and what it is not.

Differences of opinion are a normal and healthy part of human relations. By resolving your differences in a reasonable manner you develop a new understanding of the individuals involved, and of the situation that has caused the disagreement. This increases both your wisdom and your capacity to communicate.

Conflict, on the other hand adds emotion to the discussion and the emotion involved is almost always anger. *You get angry when you feel threatened or feel that you are going to lose something.* This is at the heart of a conflicting situation. It is important to change a conflict into a difference of opinion because when anger conflicts with reason, anger invariably wins. Although this rarely results in violence, these solutions will usually be achieved at the expense of reason and it is important to remember that *an effective life is guided by reason.* Therefore the first step in solving conflict is to identify what is seen as under attack or being lost.

Conflict occurs among individuals and the groups they form. Although there are many *apparent* reasons for the anger that underlies conflict (as opposed to pure disagreement), the root cause is generally the fear that one of the following is going to happen:

(a) Real or imagined loss of power

(b) Real or imagined loss of value

Although each of these is sometimes the *sole* cause of conflict, they are usually closely related, as are their solutions. Your value is often measured in terms of the influence you wield. The greater your influence the more value you perceive you have. When either are challenged, you will resist and reason will usually suffer.

There are three ways that most people deal with conflict. You can "eliminate" conflict by the arbitrary use of power. *"I'm your husband (boss, major customer etc) – do it."* Or, you can *avoid* the problem completely either by diffusing the issue, pretending it's not really a problem or hoping it will go away. Unfortunately, solutions based on power generally aggravate the conflict, making subsequent solutions more difficult. Solutions based on avoidance are generally overtaken by events that force unpleasant solutions that might have been avoided by earlier positive action. The most effective way of dealing with conflict is to protect, and if possible, enhance the power and/or value of those affected. There are four ways that this can be accomplished:

– *Understanding.* Search actively and objectively for all the facts governing the issue, and express a *genuine* understanding of the other person's point of view. Put yourself rationally *and* emotionally in their shoes. You may not agree with them, but that is not the issue.

– *Acceptance of value.* Let the other person know that their opinion has merit. Listen to them, clarify your understanding of their position, and acknowledge its positive aspects. Acceptance of value often implies accepting or reassigning part of the blame for the conflict. For example, *"I know that there are many other factors that contribute to this," "I think that I was partially to blame for the difficulty in communication," "I don't think that our Mr. Baker took all the circumstances into account."* By reassigning part of the blame or eliminating the question of blame, you are withdrawing the implied threat to the other person's value.

– *Body language.* The body language that you use is vital in the resolution of conflict. Smile, lean forward, open your arms, look understandingly into the other person's eyes and adopt a thoughtful, non-challenging body pose and a soft voice. These are all essential in conveying to the other person that neither their power nor their value is being threatened or eroded.

– *Transfer of power.* If one cause of conflict is a perceived loss of power, then a resolution involves a reduction of that threat by transferring power back to the conflicted person.

"What would you like me to do?" "This is what you can do," "Have you considered this?" "Can you help me?" – "What do you suggest?" "I'm not able to do this but this is how you can."

Remember that genuine agreement and compromise are not negative, as they are the results of a positive and developing programme of four component parts, none of which can be ignored. They are: *understanding, cooperation, a flexible use of power and a mutual and expressed appreciation of value.*

THE ART OF GRACE

Grace is a subtle quality that expresses an individual's deep belief in civilized and rational behaviour. People who practise the art of grace believe that as a species we possess superior qualities that allow us to appreciate the finer aspects of human life, qualities that raise us substantially and definitively above other animals and which enable us to plan for more durable and comfortable means of survival. Included in these qualities is the ability to be guided by a sense of what is rational and reasonable rather than by purely emotional and intuitive responses. We have discussed in an earlier paragraph the need to be guided by reason.

Individuals who practise the art of grace do so from a sense of moral, ethical and social obligation, believing that this will elevate and harmonize both their lives and the lives of those around them. They have the ability to rise above their own limited perceptions by being objective and flexible in their opinions and not dogmatically tied to them. Individuals who practise this strive to face life with a noble mind, a generous heart and a forgiving spirit. They are concerned with people rather than things, and in being motivated by the loftier ideals of compromise, compassion and understanding are not petty, malicious or vengeful.

SOME COMMON ERRORS IN OUR
BELIEF SYSTEM ABOUT OTHERS

1. When other people's feelings are hurt I have to hold myself responsible *OR ELSE* I am not a loving person.

2. Most people must be watched most of the time *OR ELSE* they will take advantage of me.

3. I must always be the peacemaker in my relationships *OR ELSE* I will be failing in my personal duty.

4. People do not usually appreciate what others do for them and *THEREFORE* I will not bother with them.

5. I must avoid expressing how I feel *OR ELSE* I may hurt other people's feelings and they won't like me.

6. People are basically selfish and only care about themselves and their own feelings and *THEREFORE* I am not going to waste my time reaching out to them.

7. I must see other people's problems as mine *OR ELSE* I am not a caring person.

8. I cannot affirm other people no matter what they do *AS IT* will make them think they are better than me.

9. I know certain people very well and *THEREFORE* I always know what they are thinking.

10. Some people are so awful that I cannot stand to be with them and *THEREFORE* I do not even try to get to know them.

11. I must reject the apologies of others *OR ELSE* they will think I am weak.

12. When others act in a way I don't like, I must avoid rather than understand them, *AS* understanding them is a waste of my time.

Exercise #9
YOUR ATTITUDE TO OTHERS

(1) Name three people with whom you have had or are having a communication breakdown.

_____

(2) In regard to each of these three persons, describe the types of situation in which the communication breakdown occurs.

(a) _____

_____

(b) _____

_____

(c) _____

_____

(3) What are your feelings about this?

_____

_____

(4) What personal behavioural change could help the situation? (i.e. better listening, greater understanding, more compassion etc)

_____

_____

(5) Can you locate the distortion in your "attitude" to others that prevents you from changing? State the distortion. (Refer to the previous list of common errors in our belief system about others)

(a) _____

_____

(b) _____

_____

(c) _____

_____

Let us now summarize the main conclusions of this chapter.

SUMMARY OF CHAPTER EIGHT

1. We need others in order to survive socially, biologically, psychologically and spiritually. It is in our interest to cultivate the good will of others in order to enhance our survival.

2. Others will intimidate us until we realize that we all have the same needs, are essentially similar and that our humanity will only grow in the soil of mutual acceptance.

3. Transform your enemies into being indifferent to you, those who are indifferent to you into friends and your friends into even better ones. You cannot afford one enemy, no matter how humble.

4. Develop the art of pleasing both the heart and the eyes.

5. Develop the art of proactive communication.

6. Develop the art of managing conflict by acknowledging and re-establishing the other side's power and value.

7. Develop the qualities of a generous heart, a forgiving spirit and a noble mind.

8. Respect for others involves cooperation, understanding, a flexible use of power and an expressed appreciation of value.

Chapter Nine

LIVING WITH THE WORLD

"The Talmud proclaims that we come into the world with clenched fists but leave it with open hands. I believe that this suggests that life requires us to hold, use and enjoy the things of the world but at the same time to remain free, unshackled and liberated from the tyranny of their ownership and control."
                                                                    Anonymous

"The grand essentials to happiness in this life are something to do, something to love and something to hope for."   *Joseph Addison*

"It is transparently obvious that an automatic rejection of the "things" of the world is not a choice but an evasion of it."   *Thomas Merton*

"What are the things of the world that we love so much, the ownership of which we proclaim with pride and defend with passion? They include our material possessions and our talents, attainments and physical gifts. Do we see these as a special trust to be used for the protection, development and uplifting of those who are weak, vulnerable and less skilled, or do we establish "ownership" of them and use that to bully, diminish and control? In simpler terms, do we use the "things" of the world for personal gain and the exploitation of others, or do we hold them in trust for their benefit?"
                                                                    Anonymous

"Love people and use things. When we reverse this by loving things and using people we are not living with the world, we are exploiting it.
                                                                    Anonymous

We live in a world of "things." Although there are some who may try to maintain a lofty detachment either emotionally, intellectually or physically from the world, the fact remains that you cannot avoid relating with other people and the things of the world that you share with them. Given this reality, let us look first at what these things are and what attitude an effective life should take in dealing with them. For example: What "things" are most important to you? Which have the most and the least value? To what lengths are you prepared to go to protect them? To what extent will you allow yourself to enjoy them? What do you mean when you assert that you own some "thing," and what is the cost and benefit of that ownership? Your understanding of the significance of these questions is vital if you are to establish an appropriate relationship with the phenomenal world around you.

The first question that must be asked is, "What are the 'things' of the world?" It is generally assumed that these consist of the material items that you either own or can in certain circumstances possess. To a limited extent this is true, but in reality there are many more. The "things" of the world include your physical, emotional and intellectual attributes, your attainments, the characteristics that you take pride in and defend, material possessions that are obtainable, and, of course, the infinitely varied environment of nature. Your attitude to the world is determined by the extent to which you regard these things as exclusively yours or as a trust, the responsibility of which you have to honour. There is a quotation from the Jewish tradition (Torah – Book of Leviticus), which in many ways suggests what this attitude should be. *"We are all born with clenched fists, but we must all die with open hands."* I think this means that we are obliged to reach out and to grasp the good things in life that are available to us *(the clenched fist of enjoyment)* but never to become so attached, dominated or directed by them that we cannot give them up *(the open hands of dispossession)*. In the humanitarian tradition this is seen as the philosophy of *possession* versus *dispossession*.

You can only *truly* enjoy the things that are available to you if that enjoyment results from a combination of pleasure and non-attachment. The above quotation continues, *"and on the Day of Judgement, we will not only be judged for the things we did that were not permitted but also for not doing the joyous things that were."*

Unfortunately within our Western religious heritage there is a strong tradition of world rejection that encourages an avoidance of worldly temptation. This tradition suggests that it is somehow immoral to enjoy the world and its pleasures and that positive enjoyment of either is a cause for guilt. Even today many traditional beliefs maintain that avoidance strengthens character and is inherently good for you, while pleasurable indulgence is at best risky and at worst sinful. I think that this is a completely spurious interpretation of the original message which was to encourage detached enjoyment and not the promotion of *world rejection.* This responsibility rests between an obligation to enjoy the world's gifts and an avoidance, *not of the gifts themselves,* but of the attachment, control and limitation of freedom that can come with them. Let us look for a moment at this *"clenched fists"* philosophy of possession and the *"open hands"* philosophy of dispossession.

Have you ever been given a gift that was not appreciated or valued? If history were ever to make a judgement of your response to the gift of life, what would that judgement be? If you were ever to be marked on how fully, how passionately and how truly you have embraced this gift, how would you measure up? I suspect that many people would get a failing grade. The world is indeed a wonderful place and we are privileged to be part of it. You can feel the joys of a sunset seen from a mountaintop so intensely that it can bring tears to your eyes, you can taste the infinite abundance of food that is available, be motivated by the pleasure of achievement, energized by the capacity of your body, delighted and mystified by the ever-advancing technologies that flood the market and each of us is mystically endowed with the hope that greater experiences will be ours. Why do we have this almost infinite capacity to enjoy and to hope for future enjoyment if there is neither the capacity nor the obligation to do so? These should be gratefully honoured by reaching out hungrily to embrace the good things of life and by eagerly anticipating the greater experiences that are within our grasp.

On the other hand, and in many ways restrictive of this ability to enjoy, are the seductive demands of ownership and possession. What is frequently overlooked when possession rather than enjoyment becomes a main goal, is that you cannot own without being owned and you cannot possess without being possessed. You may own a house but your house possesses an owner and that ownership imposes significant obligations. A man may have a wife, children and worldly assets, but his wife also has a husband, his children have a father and the assets an owner, and he is obliged to protect them all. All the things you own possess you as much as you possess them and impose obligations upon you. It is imperative that these be seen as part of, and as the price of, ownership. Have you ever had a friend who was possessive of you and who demanded of you more than you were prepared or able to give? A friend who insisted that their problems become your problems, who drained all your energy and restricted your freedom? Eventually, if you were wise, that friendship had to be evaluated in terms of your needs and obligations, and if necessary, discarded. It is this type of evaluation that you should apply to all the things of the world that can very easily begin to control you and limit your freedom.

This evaluation should be for the purpose of creating a balance between enjoying the good things of the world and a desire not to be controlled and led by them. It will help to maintain that balance if you look carefully at those "things" which are really important to you and the sacrifices you make to maintain that importance. It helps to relate your love of things to the individuals around you and to see how your attitudes to these are balanced. Are there some "things" in your life that are more important than the people in it? Your career, for example, the admiration of your friends, or the power and responsibility you wield in the workplace? When it comes to a choice between protecting the important "things" in your life and the interests of the "people" who are part of it, which choice are you usually inclined to make and where does your emotional commitment lie? There is an old saying, *"Where your treasure is hidden, there you will hide your heart."* What do you treasure most and for what do you save your heart? Do you *"love things and use people"* to further that commitment or are you wise enough to reverse this and *"love people and use things?"*

I have said earlier that a truly effective life is born in the soil of self-love and grows into a genuine and unconditional love of others. To what extent does your love and ownership of "things" tempt you to invert the principle: *"love people, use things?"* How did you establish "ownership" of your strengths in the first place? It is said quite correctly that you were "given" most of your inherent qualities at birth and as such your relationship with them should be viewed as a temporary trust rather than one of exclusive ownership. Are you so proud of your intellect, wit, physical strength, good looks or background that you bully, manipulate and eventually weaken those around you to prove and maintain that ownership? Or do you use your "gifts" for the benefit and growth of those who are weaker and less blessed?

Most psychologists will tell you that in every relationship there is one who is generally emotionally or physically stronger than the other. The truly effective person sees their strength as an ethical obligation to be used to encourage the growth, security and self-esteem of the other. Unfortunately, however, it is often used to abuse, and in its more subtle forms to manipulate, control and intimidate, a sure sign that it is the "thing" that is valued and not the person. In his wonderful book, *People of the Lie*, M. Scott Peck brings to life the many variations of this type of individual, who in their most pronounced form are very evil.

Let us look at some of the many ways in which some people may encounter and be challenged by the choice between an ethical relationship with others *(loving people)* and the need to protect and proclaim those things in life which have them hooked *(loving things)*.

For example, a person's proclaimed *qualities of character:* do these truly represent their inner character and their values or were they conveniently created because they look good? In other words, how authentic are they? Individuals, for example, who maintain proudly that they always have the courage of their convictions and who rarely change their minds, forget that this is the basis of bigotry. Most people believe in their convictions and by itself this is not really a big deal. *An effective life has the courage to reject those convictions when they don't measure up to rational logic.* Flexibility in viewpoint, attitude, and personal need is often far more conducive to a happy, effective life than a more unyielding and *seemingly* stronger approach. *"The birch tree bends but doesn't break; the oak tree breaks because it cannot bend"* is an old adage that contains much wisdom.

Do you pride yourself on your reputation for friendliness? How do you express that, at what cost and more importantly, why? Many families are devastated by a tyrannical father or a controlling mother whose desire to impress others and to gain their affection is at the expense of genuinely loving a family whose affection was taken for granted or not needed.

What do you do, for example, if you pride yourself on loyalty and a long-term employee to whom you are loyal competes for promotion with a more qualified employee who is not entitled to the same obligation? *Are you "hooked" by your loyalty or guided by the more stringent requirements of ethical leadership?*

What about your achievements, gifts or talents? To a limited extent, the things you acquire by personal effort and your special talents do tend to produce a feeling of superiority. A qualified accountant, lawyer or doctor does have greater financial, legal or medical knowledge than a layman. A sharp and incisive mind, a commanding intellect and a natural facility with the use of words all carry very specific benefits in society, but balance demands that they also carry obligations. Wisdom and talent imply power, but power married to proprietary pride is a dangerous partnership, especially when it is also matched with other, less obvious but weaker qualities such as low self-esteem, a need to control or hypersensitivity. How do you use the "power" derived from your "wisdom" and talent? If you are a lawyer for example, and a close friend needs informal legal advice, do you intimidate by direction and control, maintaining your friend's submissive status, or do you guide, suggest and enlighten?

In other words, where others are concerned do you use your knowledge, strength or talent to empower or to weaken, to encourage or deter, to liberate or to control, to enlighten or to obscure? The difference has profound implications. In their relationships with women for example, men are often criticized for being *problem solvers* rather than *solution facilitators*. Again problem solvers tend to weaken and to control others, solution facilitators empower and liberate. How do you use the power, vested in you by your achievements, to solve the problems of others?

What about your *background?* So often a character weakness, personal inadequacy or basic insecurity can hide behind a cloak of national, religious, racial or social pride and then be used as a tool of control and manipulation. For example:

"I come from a harsh background so I'm entitled to act in this way to you. You should understand that."

"I'm from a repressed minority, you should give me special favours."

"My religious tradition will not allow me to act in the way that I would like."

Religious, racial, social and cultural traditions are certainly an important part of your identity and mould your thoughts and feelings. As such they can be significant guides to the behaviour that a secure society needs and expects, but these traditions can also exploit you, victimize you, control you and limit your freedom. When they do this they frequently force you to either betray your own developing sense of ethics, eliminate them totally or provide you with a seductive opportunity to evade rather than to challenge your weaknesses. Your daughter is in love with and wants to marry someone from another faith. Do you love your "thing" (your faith) or do you love your child? Do you allow consciousness of your colour to cloud your judgement when dealing with others who have not suffered from prejudice? You have a poor and underprivileged background. Does this control your work habits, your ambition and your desire to "get on in the world" so much that the needs of your family are neglected? If so, and in each of these examples, you are being led, controlled and victimized by the limitations of your background instead of being guided by your aspirations, needs and values.

Now let us look finally at the more obvious things of the world, material possessions. We live in an acquisitive society, whose members are frequently defined by the ownership of physical goods. The need to own and to enjoy that ownership is an essential part of our human nature, and to deny it denies that reality. Every individual is defined by the effort they expend in order to survive. That effort is energized, justified and evaluated by what it produces for the use and enjoyment of the individual. That use is generally defined by ownership. Any society that has attempted to change this paradigm has generally failed. This being the case, it is imperative that you carefully determine the priorities and significance of the things you own and want and the effort and sacrifices you are willing to make for them. This stringent analysis must be applied to *everything* that you own or want to own. If you do this and act rationally upon it, you will enjoy ownership and possession. If you do not, and if you let fear and insecurity take over, your desire for bigger and greater possessions will never be satisfied. Unfortunately, in order to feed and encourage an unexamined pursuit of ownership, our society is being intentionally made ever more fearful and insecure about life itself. Take a moment to examine any newspaper and you will see that in most cases the pervading message is that life is *inherently* dangerous and that the pursuit of material comforts will insulate you from or mitigate that danger.

Which of your possessions encourages you to invert the principle, *"Love people, use things?"* If, for example, your three-year-old child calls you over to the dining room table to admire her latest watercolour painting, do you ignore for the moment the paint stains on the tablecloth and compliment her or is your *first* reaction to tell her to be careful or to complain about her carelessness? If your teenager phones to tell you that he has smashed the fender of your car, what is your *first* reaction? Is it "How are you?" or "What's the extent of the damage?" If the expense of buying the new 3,000 square foot house involves less money for family vacations or more time at work away from the children, which takes priority, the new house or the family?

Every possession involves sacrifice and commitment. If after careful thought you consider that the price of ownership for a particular possession is too high or that there are more important priorities, and *if you still persist in pursuit of that ownership*, it's fairly safe to say that you do not own your possession, it owns you and you have compromised your freedom of action.

SOME COMMON ERRORS IN OUR BELIEF SYSTEM ABOUT THE WORLD

1. I must obtain recognition for my personal attainments *OR ELSE* I will not feel like much of a person.

2. The world is a source of temptation and I must avoid these temptations *OR ELSE* I will be corrupted.

3. The world of nature does not really benefit me *SO* I try to avoid it as much as possible.

4. I must get as much as I can in this world *OR ELSE* the competition will get my share.

5. My physical gifts are purely biological and I *THEREFORE* have no right to take a delight in them.

6. I must ignore my positive attributes or talents *OR ELSE* I will forget my faults and become selfish and conceited.

7. As I cannot take anything with me I must reject the enjoyable gifts of life *OR ELSE* I will get too attached to them.

8. I must have certain material possessions *OR ELSE* I will not be happy or fulfilled.

9. I must surround myself by more and more material comforts *OR ELSE* I will not feel secure.

Final exercises in this chapter will take an honest look at some of your favourite things and the extent that they may direct or control you. To assist you in completing these exercises, it is important to bear in mind once again that it is not only the material things in your world that can control you but also your attainments and qualities. When they do, there is often an observable shift in the impact they can have on your life (from positive to negative). Unfortunately, this shift is more likely to be observed by those around you than by yourself.

Loyalty, for example, can become slavish devotion, independence can change into a selfish toughness of character, enduring friends can become doormats, friendliness can decline into a self-sacrificing search for approval, honesty can descend into a self-proclaiming righteousness, wisdom can become an intellectual and inflexible arrogance and courage in one's personal convictions can be transformed into unyielding dogma.

The exercise on the next page will help you identify your attitude to various "things" of the world.

Exercise #10

These are a few of my favourite things:

My Natural Qualities of Character

List some of your innate qualities of which you are proud, such as being loyal, independent, enduring, friendly or honest.

In what way are you tempted to proclaim and defend these qualities and what personal and social sacrifices do you make in doing so? Does this in any way invert the principle, *"Love people, use things?"*

My Attainments

List some of those things that you have achieved by personal effort, such as your university degree, professional qualification, reputation, professional position, circle of friends or wisdom.

In what way are you tempted to invert the principle, *"Love people, use things"*, by proclaiming and defending the above attainments?

My Physical Gifts and Talents

List some of the physical qualities or talents that you are proud of. For example: height, appearance, build, looks, strength, personality or charisma.

_____

In what way are you tempted to invert the principle, _"Love people, use things"_, by proclaiming and defending these qualities and talents? Do you use them for the benefit or detriment of others?

_____

_____

_____

My Background

What are the aspects of your background that are important to you and which you defend and proclaim? For example: race, colour, religion, cultural tradition or economic/social origins.

_____

In what way are you tempted to invert the principle, _"Love people, use things"_, by proclaiming and defending your background? How often do you rely on your background to "escape" from personal responsibility? Manipulate others? Avoid recognizing personal limitations?

_____

_____

My Material Possessions

List some of the things that you own that are *very* important to you, such as your house, car, stereo equipment, stocks and securities or jewellery, etc.

_____

_____

In what ways do you invert the principle, *"Love people, use things"*, by aspiring to, obtaining and retaining the above? What personal and social sacrifices do you make to do so? Do these things really merit these sacrifices?

_____

_____

_____

In reviewing the above "things" that you consider important (qualities of character, attainments, physical gifts or talents, background and possessions), it is wise to reflect for a moment on the questions that you initially asked about them.

What are the most important things in your life?

_____

How do you prioritize them? What criteria do you use in doing so?

_____

What effort and sacrifices do you make in order to keep, enhance and preserve them?

Does anyone suffer as a result of those sacrifices? If so, who?

Are these "things" worth the sacrifices that you make for them?

If not, why are you so committed to making them?

Think carefully about your answers and review them in conjunction with the list of attitude distortions mentioned previously. If you detect a limitation in any area, consider using the principles of S.A.F.E.R. and C.M.E.A. to correct it.

Before looking at an appropriate attitude to life, let us summarize the main points of chapter nine.

SUMMARY OF CHAPTER NINE

1. The world contains many "things" which can be used for enjoyment and pleasure.

2. These things not only include food and material things, but talents, qualities of character, physical gifts and attainments.

3. An appropriate relationship to the things of the world should be governed by detached enjoyment rather than controlling need.

4. An effective relationship with the things of the world should be strongly guided by a reasoned scrutiny of their importance, the sacrifices made to obtain and maintain them and an appreciation of the effects of their influence.

5. A further guide is an awareness of the degree to which this relationship is governed by the dictum, *"Love people and use things"* rather than its alternative, *"Love things and use people."*

6. The inappropriate influence of "things" that are loved is demonstrated when their controlling influence outweighs the positive aspect of their enjoyment.

7. If the need to proclaim, defend or obtain knowledge, skill or material wealth is a controlling one, the process of S.A.F.E.R. and C.M.E.A. as outlined in Vision Renaissance should be used to isolate and replace the attitude limitation that predicates this control.

Chapter Ten

LIVING WITH LIFE

"It is not the critic who counts, nor the man who points out where the strong man has stumbled, nor where the doer of deeds could have done them better. On the contrary, the credit belongs to the man who is actually in the arena, whose vision is marred by dust and sweat and blood; who strives valiantly; who errs frequently and who comes back again and again; who knows great devotions, great enthusiasms and glorious passions and who at best knows in the end the triumph of his achievement. However, if he fails, if he fails, at least he fails greatly so that his place shall never be with those cold and timid souls who know neither victory nor defeat."   *Teddy Roosevelt*

"Learn from yesterday, live for today, hope for tomorrow."   *Anonymous*

"Enjoy life. There's plenty of time to be dead."   *Anonymous*

"Life consists not in holding good cards but in playing those you hold well."   *Richard Bach*

"The question is not whether we will die, but whether we will live."   *Anonymous*

"Believe that life is worth living and your belief will help create the fact."   *Oliver Wendell Holmes*

"The tragedy of life is not that it ends so soon, but that we wait so long to begin it."   *William James*

"Live every day as if it were your last, because one of these days, it will be."   *Albert Camus*

"Love and forgive as if there were no yesterday, live as if you would die tomorrow.

Plan as though you would live forever."   *Millard Fuller*

"Fear not that your life will have an end. Fear rather that it will not have a beginning."   *Cardinal Newman*

"You cannot run away from a weakness; you must sometime fight it out or perish. This being the case, why not now, and where you stand?"
          Anonymous

"Nothing will ever be attempted if at first all possible objections must be overcome."   *Samuel Johnson*

The steps leading to a life-enhancing interpretation of reality can be clearly identified. A belief that is unconditionally self-loving and self-accepting develops into an effective relationship with others and the world of things. This wider vision is then guided by various life principles which determine the choices we make.

Let us look initially at what is an appropriate *life principle* and if you find a significant difference between this description and your own, it is suggested that you consider applying the principles of Vision Renaissance. A "life principle" has been defined as:

> *"A generally accepted purpose in living that is applied to, directs and underlies the specific choices that we make in life"*

Here are some of the more toxic beliefs that many people hold and which influence the life principles that govern their actions. Ask yourself honestly whether any of these are part of your belief system and significantly influence the way you behave. Look at them from the position of what your feelings tell you rather than your thoughts as our thoughts can often lead us away from the objective honesty that this demands.

SOME COMMON ERRORS IN
OUR BELIEF SYSTEM ABOUT LIFE

1. Early events in my life determine my present circumstances and behaviour and *THEREFORE* there is little possibility of growth or change.

2. *AS* I have only one life I must grab as many of life's pleasures as often as I can.

3. I must know the territory in my endeavours *OR ELSE* I will be in danger of failing or things might happen that I will not like.

4. Success and happiness are generally determined by external circumstances and *THEREFORE* I have little control over my life.

5. I must never forget that the most important thing in life is to have fun *OR ELSE* I may lose out on it.

6. Where possible, I must influence the activities of others *OR ELSE* they and events will control me.

7. I must accept my personal limitations and background *OR ELSE* I will find life frustrating and unfulfilling.

8. Life is unjust to me *BECAUSE* so many others were born with greater advantages.

9. I must be happy most of the time *OR ELSE* life will be unfair.

10. I must direct others who are close to me in their actions *OR ELSE* I will be failing in my duty to protect them.

11. I'm just a small and insignificant cog in a universe that I cannot control, *THEREFORE* I must accept whatever comes my way in life.

12. I must find out how to be happy *OR ELSE* I will miss out on life's greatest secret.

13. Where possible, I must have things done my way *OR ELSE* I am reluctant to become fully involved.

14. I must avoid the risk of pain, anxiety or rejection as much as possible *OR ELSE* I won't get my full share of happiness.

15. I must constantly remember the past and plan for the future, *AS* without this, I cannot control the inherent dangers of the present.

16. *AS* I only have a limited time available I must cram into it as many experiences as I possibly can.

17. Life is full of unforeseen obstacles *THEREFORE* I must be extra cautious in approaching it.

The major life principles that motivate our actions are directly influenced by three *vitally* important factors: (1) our basic trust in life (2) our ability to accept the uncertainties of it and (3) our attitude towards time. In Chapter Two, I described the importance of an appropriate attitude to time so let us now look at trust and uncertainty.

TRUSTING LIFE

Trust can be defined as *"a firm belief in the ultimate strength, truth, reliability and benevolence of something."* This belief is a vital part of the attitude that we each hold towards life. *Our main struggle in life is the choice that we must all constantly make between a proactive quest for living and a reactive avoidance of pain.* A basic trust in life itself is generally how we can resolve that conflict.

I indicated in Chapter One that an initial trust in the world around us is basic to the development of an authentic "self", as it allows us to embrace life with its risks and uncertainties. This trust is generally governed by three factors: a belief that we are free to act in the first place, the degree of security we feel in doing so and an *intuitive belief that the worst is not likely to happen.* The last of these arises from a basic belief that life and the world are organized and operate in our favour. Traditionally, this psychological need has been filled by religious faith, which, although often condemned by rationalists, fills a vital human need that cannot be ignored in any valid model of personal growth.

Unfortunately faith has been traditionally based on an *unreasoning* and *unquestioning* belief in a superior being who is ultimately *controlling* and frequently *vengeful.* The obvious inadequacies of this have undermined our trust and faith without eliminating our psychological need for it. In our modern age, I believe that our need for a basic trust in life can be at least minimally met by a *rationally* based belief in an *organizing life principle*, which is basically *constructive* and *integrating.* What then is this organizing life principle that may meet this basic criteria?

There is indisputable scientific evidence that we live in a universe guided by intricate and organized design and we see this evidence everywhere. In neutrons, electrons and protons as they practise their mystical and yet disciplined dance within the confines of a lonely atom. In the awesome wonder of a billion planets, stars and solar systems moving obediently to the same intricate pattern as the atom, identical in design and differing only in immensity. We see it in life itself as it develops from cell to psyche in an organized and structured pattern of conception, birth, growth, decay and death and we see it daily in the self-adjusting healing faculties of the human body which are automatically triggered when an organism is damaged and turned off when it is no longer needed.

The issue is not whether these principles of design and organization have a purpose, but whether you believe that they exist. To suggest that life has neither an organizing principle nor design is to sabotage life itself. As we stand in awe before what is unknown and unknowable our growth depends upon trusting its ultimate benevolence.

> *Let us face life with a trust in its ultimate goodness. Whether that trust rests in an all-knowing spirit or in blue skies, green fields, rugged mountains, smiling flowers and rolling seas, let us stand in awe before its beauty, mystery and wonder.*
>
> *Let us declare an undying trust in the benevolent progress of life because everything that we think, feel and do is ultimately an act of trust, and it is that which powers our growth.*
>
> *Let us develop in our life a passion for whatever comes. However dark our horizons may be, however overcast our own personal skies, however rough our own road, let us face life with courage, endurance and faith in our personal will, for adversity will always be defeated by personal courage, obstacles will always break on the anvil of endurance and no power on earth can resist a will that is prepared to sacrifice itself in order to live and experience.*
>
> *Let us finally take a chance on life by trusting in our own will and strength, knowing that even if we are buffeted by the winds of unforeseen misfortune we would have given life itself a chance.*

Although, in our enlightened age many people have lost confidence in the irrational dogma of religion, the limitations of science and the illusion of political utopias, this must not shake our basic trust in life itself. It doesn't really matter whether this rests upon a divine being, the beauty of nature, or the unique unfolding panorama of its growth, or whether it results in pain or joy. Let us trust life and worship at its altar because trust creates hope, optimism, growth and health and it is a lack of trust that creates despair, pessimism, decline and disease.

UNCERTAINTY

Trusting in the ultimate benevolence of life leads to a genuine acceptance of uncertainty but it is obvious that the future cannot be predicted. Many people try to prove that they can do so however, by programming their lives in the frustrating and impossible pursuit of certainty. The *"what if"* individual, for example, who constantly delays decisions by planning for all eventualities hoping they can both predict and forestall every negative event; the worrier who believes that negative future events can be magically transformed by experiencing pain in advance; controlling individuals who believe that organizing those around them will achieve the same effect; and dreamers who prefer dreaming to the more uncertain results of action. All are trying to escape the reality of uncertainty and the pain that it may bring. The problems that may arise from unforeseen challenges and experiences are a legitimate and necessary part of life itself, and attempting to escape from them is an escape from living. As Carl Jung so wisely put it, *"Neurosis is a substitute for legitimate suffering."* Uncertainty is an inevitable fact of life because of three factors:

1) The world changes, often unpredictably, and usually because of actions that you do not perform yourself.

2) Even when the world does not change, your opinions of it do, especially when you receive new evidence and information.

3) Your beliefs about the world and upon which you act may be uncertain, incorrect, biased or inappropriate and these will naturally produce unforeseen results.

Influencing your ability to accept uncertainty is the *apparent* conflict between free will and fate, and the belief that these are incompatible. It is suggested that if your life is solely determined by fate you have no freedom of action, and if it is not, you have the sole and awesome responsibility for *all* of your actions.

By themselves each of these beliefs will limit your ability to act by encouraging either a passive and reactive personality, or an excessively cautious one. Fused together, however, they will enhance your ability to proactively control those aspects of your life that you can control and to accept with mature wisdom those you cannot. Free will and fate are both compatible and *necessary.* Although you may have little control over many of the events that happen to you, you do have significant control over how you deal with them. As quoted at the beginning of this chapter, *"Life consists not in holding good cards but in playing those you hold well."*

The need to control the events in your life in order to avoid uncertainty stems from an inherent need to be secure. A basic trust in life and in your ability to make rational decisions within an uncertain environment begins the process of replacing the comfort of non-action with the potential discomfort of action. It is then that we start to grow. To put it more subtly: *The greatest possible security that you can possess is the ability to accept insecurity.* Let us now turn to *your* attitude to life.

In thinking about *your* own general attitude to life, it often helps to look at your "feelings" and your "gut" responses rather than just relying on your thoughts. Quite often, when you only "think" things through, you tend to come out with memorized and habitual answers that often fail to reflect what you really feel at a deeper level. Every individual has a different way of reacting to those deeper feelings.

Let us look for a moment at the *meaning* of your life. If someone were to ask you, "What does life *mean* to you?" what would be your initial "gut" response? Is it an adventure or a struggle? An opportunity for growth or an obstacle to be overcome? Do you embrace life or endure it?

Would your feelings, on the other hand, suggest that it's a painful experience or a pleasurable one, a series of hidden expectations or unexpected heartaches? What do the challenges of life do to you? Do they strengthen or weaken you? Motivate your desire to grow or discourage it, instil courage or fear? If you were asked to write a life script for yourself beginning with, "I will be a success if I - - -," what would the script say and what would those values indicate? Do you wake up and say "Good morning God?" Or do you groan and say, "Good God, it's morning?" Finally, and before we discuss an appropriate attitude to life, please review the questions above and try to develop a general feeling for how you see your life. You need not be too specific as all you are doing at this stage is developing an awareness of what motivates your effort, priorities and ambition. You may, for instance, believe that money is most important, or perhaps fame, approval, influence or having a good time. There are others who are motivated almost exclusively by the need to make themselves secure.

Most people, however, are primarily motivated by one of three guiding principles, each of which are developed by the degree to which they trust life and accept uncertainty. These motivators of human nature are: *Pleasure, Power* and the *Avoidance of Responsibility.* Generally, however, one of them is stronger and provides the life principle, which underwrites an individual's actions. *An effective life fuses these three principles together and is guided by their value and utility. The ineffective life is controlled by them and is driven by their addictive influence and demands.*

> *An effective attitude to life will only be achieved when you recognize those things which motivate you to action and when you are guided by their value and personal utility rather than driven by their power and demands.*

Let us now look in detail at these three powerful motivators and how they affect our life. In traditional psychology, Sigmund Freud postulated that human beings are motivated mainly by a desire for pleasure. Subsequent theorists maintained that additional to this was the need for power and influence resulting from our insecurity in an uncertain environment, and others still that this uncertainty created a need to avoid personal responsibility. Traditionally, this latter need was achieved by placing responsibility for our actions upon fate or a supreme being.

In reality, however, we are motivated by both power, pleasure and avoidance but one usually dominates and this then becomes a guiding life principle modified by the other two.

A guiding life principle is developed for reasons of psychological economy. If we have two conflicting decisions and our life principle is pleasure, our decision will be based on where we will have greater pleasure. If our choice is between two job opportunities and we are motivated by power, our choice will be the one which carries the most influence, quite possibly ignoring its disadvantages. If our life principle is one of avoidance, we will be motivated to blame our difficulties upon circumstances rather than our own inadequacy.

Almost all great traditions maintain that an effective life can only really be achieved when each of these three motivators are fused together in such a way that they *guide you by their value and utility* instead of *controlling you by their power and demands.* Before looking at how this can be done, let us look at how each of these three life principles operates in a practical setting and how their *uncontrolled* dominating influence can negatively affect your life.

THE PURSUIT OF PLEASURE

I have suggested in the previous chapter that our world is full of things to enjoy and it is our duty to do so, but we must at the same time maintain the freedom to do so and not be their servant. We should be defined by our free ability to choose and to bear the consequences of choice, and when we fail to do this our capacity to enjoy is diminished. *It is only our freedom to choose that gives us the capacity to fully enjoy.*

We constantly see individuals whose freedom has been curtailed by the seductive and gradually addictive demands of pleasure where initial attraction has been quickly followed by desire, need and finally by sacrifice. Let us look at some obvious examples. Eating well-cooked and tasty food is one of life's great pleasures. Unchecked, however, this can gradually become addictive, as evidenced by the frequency of obesity, diabetes and heart trouble. Alcohol is an undeniable pleasure for many, but alcoholics often make terrible sacrifices of family, career and finances when they lose control. Sexual pleasure is one of our greatest gifts and should be enjoyed to the full, but how often do we meet individuals whose lives have been ruined by the need for wider and more frequent sexual experience? How often the glutton, alcoholic and libertine must secretly long for the days when food, wine and sexual intimacy were genuine, longed-for delights rather than commanding needs?

THE PURSUIT OF POWER

The second major principle that guides human action is the desire for power, influence and control. The psychologist Alfred Adler postulated that for the first fourteen or fifteen years of our life we are totally dependent upon others for our needs. As a result of this we spend the rest of it over-compensating by trying to dominate, influence and control other people and our environment. Although this may be an exaggeration, it is certainly a major influencing factor. This is understandable, as the greater control you have, the more secure you feel. The reality of the matter, however, is that you have little control over many of the major aspects of your life and no direct control over future events as they unfold. You have almost unlimited control as to how you interpret those events but not the events themselves.

We also frequently see individuals whose compulsive quest for personal power damages those around them and ultimately themselves. Quite frequently these individuals and their actions are less obvious than would appear, and as mentioned earlier, are chillingly described in M. Scott Peck's insightful book, *People of the Lie.* The controlling mother, for example, who under the guise of looking after her children's interests, controls and disempowers them, is no less damaging than the boss who bullies his staff into submission, the public servant or uniformed official who insists unreasonably on bureaucratic observance of minor rules and the friend who uses your friendship to achieve a hidden agenda. Not only do these people diminish those around them, but also, their attempts at control generally leave them with *less* perceived control and increasing isolation.

As with an obsessive pursuit of pleasure, a compulsive need to control usually increases the feeling of being out of control, which then generates an increasing need for it. (Power should only be exercised when it is necessary, rational and humane to do so and only then as a free exercise of choice and with great caution.) Most controlling individuals are actually trying to avoid the unknown by controlling the known. In so doing they are attempting a form of escape from the normal risks associated with healthy growth. As mentioned earlier, Carl Jung wrote, *"Neurosis is a substitute for legitimate suffering."* Indeed we might even suggest that *neurosis results when you try to escape from the legitimate pain of growth.* Excessive control is one of those escapes. The secret of a just use of power is in *freely* choosing that which you can and should influence, a mature acceptance of that which you cannot, and the wisdom to know the difference.

AVOIDANCE OF RESPONSIBILTY

Let us look finally at the third of our life's principles, avoidance of responsibility. It has been suggested that because of the rapid advancement of modern technology and the uncontrolled horror of two world wars, we have lost much of our faith in our ability to control events. This is reflected in an ever-increasing tendency to blame others and avoid personal responsibility for our actions. The media constantly encourages this belief. A recession, for example, is blamed on inefficient government planning rather than the cycles of a free economy; cancer is the fault of profiteering food companies who fill our foods with chemicals and not an individual's food choices; rising crime is caused by over-aggressive or under-efficient police forces rather than criminal irresponsibility and low incomes are blamed on corporate greed, discrimination or high taxation rather than an individual's lack of hard work and sacrifice and how they make their decisions.

The world is portrayed as *inherently* dangerous, fearful and out of control. We constantly hear tales that the medical system is falling apart, that food is chemically poisoned, that life-destroying bacteria lurks constantly for new victims and that our streets are infested with criminals. This constant negative input erodes belief in personal action and responsibility, and we have seen in the past the often-terrifying effect of this form of social inertia.

In fact, however, our world is generally safer, richer, cleaner, healthier and politically more secure than at any time before. Longevity is generally increasing, streets are safer, and democratic and liberal institutions are now standards rather than exceptions. In those unfortunate areas of our world where death and anguish are an everyday experience, the daily challenge is not with the *neurotic* fear of *imaginary* anguish but with the much *healthier* challenge of facing real problems by action.

The desire to avoid responsibility for personal action is influenced by the fatalistic view that, because you have very little control over the major events of your life, you are not responsible for the choices you make in regard to them. This is spurious, as, although you may have little control over the major parameters of your life you have a lot of control within them. For example, you can do nothing about the inherited genes that influence your health, but there is much that you can do about the food you eat, the beliefs you adopt, the exercise you do and the alcohol and nicotine you ingest. More people die of premature death from these than from poor genes. Your income is certainly influenced by your parent's wealth and cultural advantage but also to an equal and perhaps greater extent by your ambition, hard work, persistence and application. Your peace of mind is influenced mainly and almost exclusively by your attitude to life, your friendships, your values and your commitments, all of which are well within your control.

It's worth mentioning again that if you are motivated by *avoidance* it will inevitably lead to either of two life-diminishing results: a tendency to avoid purposeful action in the belief that, *"If I do nothing, I can't be blamed,"* or irresponsible actions based on a belief that nothing is your fault. Conversely, individuals who accept freedom of choice and personal responsibility generally act proactively and in a morally ethical manner.

It is not being suggested that we are *always* fully responsible for *all* the things that happen in our life, but that we are *primarily* responsible for *most* of them, and *fully* responsible for our beliefs regarding *all* of them. When you believe and practise this, you are asserting your freedom and your ability to grow and to develop a fully effective life. It is our ability to make voluntary rather than purely instinctive choices and to accept the responsibility and results of them that defines our species. It is important, however, to maintain a reasoned balance between (a) the acceptance of responsibility for our actions and (b) a mature acceptance of those situations where we cannot act. In a previous chapter I outlined the profound difference between problems that can be solved by action and those situations that have to be endured by mature acceptance. Understanding the difference is vital because they each demand different skills.

A happy and effective life can only be achieved when the three major motivators of power, pleasure or avoidance are balanced, and when they guide rather than control our actions. When this does not happen our freedom is diminished. Even in the societies that we create, history clearly demonstrates that there is a clear tendency to power in the growth stage of a culture, leading to pleasure when it has consolidated that power and eventual decline caused by avoidance. At any moment cultures generally reflect their predisposition to one or the other.

Why do some people become controlled instead of guided by one of these three life principles? In Chapter One I described how a trust in your personal ability to make life-enhancing decisions develops the self-esteem that accepts responsibility for them. What is not realized, however, is that the reverse is equally true, in that the active pursuit and acceptance of personal responsibility enhances your personal trust and self-esteem.

As mentioned earlier, the degree to which you are either guided or controlled by pleasure, power or avoidance is strongly influenced by the attitude you have towards *time, uncertainty* and *trust.* In Chapter Two, the importance of making an ally rather than an enemy of time was discussed, and we will summarize our main observations regarding this once again. If you see time as something limited and limiting, you will challenge it by trying to use it before "it runs out." Time, of course, doesn't run anywhere and neither is it limited, as both are relative to a given moment's experience. In describing time to some male students Albert Einstein wisely commented, *"If you put your hand on a hot stove for a minute it seems like an hour. If you sit with a pretty girl for an hour it seems like a minute."*

The frenetic pursuit of pleasure and experience in the belief that time is running out, is progressively demanding, possessive and finally totally consuming and the cause of much of today's stress. Taking time to smell the roses is not just a platitude; it is of fundamental importance to our growth and psychological development and directly affects our capacity for pleasure.

An inability to accept uncertainty directly affects our attitude to *power* because our need for security will encourage us to try to exercise control.

Finally, a lack of trust in the organized benevolence of life will encourage an *avoidance of responsibility* that will either discourage action or prevent it being guided by ethical and moral responsibility.

The following questions require you to think about *your* life principle and its possible controlling influence. In each area this can manifest in the following ways:

POWER

Search for Recognition • Desire for praise • Overly competitive personality • Manipulative • Authoritarian • Reluctance to be led • Hypersensitivity to criticism • Expressed need always to be included • Name-dropping and use of talents and skills to control rather than to develop, nurture or protect others

PLEASURE

Short-term goals • Follower • Immature • Negligent • Irresponsible • Unconcerned with results • Excessive sensual gratification • Sees personal needs as a priority • Unconcerned with the needs of others • Inability to use time effectively

AVOIDANCE OF RESPONSIBILITY

Indecisiveness • Reticence • Procrastination • Blaming others • Searching for a scapegoat • Lack of resolution • Limited goal-setting or future planning • Seeing self as a "victim" • Excessive caution • Dreamer • Excessive planning • Over scrupulosity • Excessive "what ifs" in decision making

Before proceeding with the following exercise, read through the above characteristics again and ask yourself whether any resonate with you as being applicable to yourself in some way. Perhaps it may help to ask a friend to also give you their objective opinion.

In answering these questions about the life principles of pleasure, power and avoidance, you should think about the personal sacrifices that you might have made in their pursuit. For example: Your personal growth, *real* needs, family and loved ones, friends, job, interests, ethical obligations and responsibilities.

This exercise demands a great deal of thoughtful introspection, so please reserve a quiet time to complete it when you are unlikely to be disturbed for at least a couple of hours.

Exercise #11:

YOUR ATTITUDE TO LIFE

1) In what way, in the last month, has the life principle of PLEA-SURE impacted negatively upon your personal growth, real needs, family and loved ones, friends, job, interests or ethical obligations and responsibilities? (Start with looking at those things that give you pleasure)

_____

_____

_____

Why? _____

_____

Can you express this in terms of a belief statement? Refer to the earlier part of this chapter for examples.

_____

_____

Try to construct a counter-logic that challenges that belief.

_____

_____

2) In what ways, in the last month, has the life principle of POW-ER impacted negatively upon your personal growth, real needs,

family and loved ones, friends, job, interests or ethical obligations and responsibilities?

_____

_____

_____

Why?_____

_____

Can you express this in terms of a belief statement? Refer to the earlier part of this chapter for examples.

_____

_____

Try to construct a counter-logic that challenges that belief.

_____

_____

3) In what ways, in the last month, has AVOIDANCE impacted negatively upon your personal growth, real needs, family and loved ones, friends, job, interests or ethical obligations?

_____

_____

_____

Why? _____

_____

Can you express this in terms of a belief statement? Refer to the earlier part of this chapter for examples.

_____

_____

Try to construct a counter-logic that challenges that belief.

_____

_____

4) Which of these three life principles (power, pleasure, avoidance of responsibility) is most tempting to you, and why?

_____

_____

_____

5) How would your life, interests and relationships be different if the above life principle did not significantly influence them?

_____

_____

_____

An effective attitude to life must include a genuine love for self, others and living. How can you develop this by changing your attitude to pleasure, power and avoidance? In this exercise each of the three life principles are applied to self, others and life.

PLEASURE

How has the life principle of pleasure affected your ability to love:

Self? _____

_____

_____

Others? _____

_____

_____

Life? _____

_____

_____

POWER

How has the life principle of power affected your ability to love:

Self? _____

_____

_____

Others? _____

_____

_____

Life? _____

_____

_____

AVOIDANCE OF RESPONSIBILITY

How has the principle of avoidance affected your ability to love:

Self? _____

_____

_____

Others? _____

_____

_____

Life? _____

_____

_____

The need to balance and to be guided by the principles of pleasure, power and the avoidance of responsibility rather than to be controlled by them is beautifully described in a short story taken from the great tradition of Indian Vedanta.

"There was once a great king who ruled his kingdom with justice and compassion. As he grew older, he became increasingly concerned over which of his four sons should rule upon his death. He eventually decided that as he wanted his people to be happy, the son who knew most about happiness should be the one to rule. Having provided each of them with unlimited resources, he dispatched them into the world with the instructions that the first son who found true happiness would inherit the kingdom.

The first son decided that happiness lay in the pursuit of pleasure, and so he built a magnificent palace, furnished with the most beautiful furniture and art that money could buy. His cellar was filled with the finest wine, his pantry with the finest food, his courtyard with the loveliest courtesans and his table was graced with the most elegant people in the land. His home became legendary for the pleasures it offered. For a while all was well and he thought he was happy, but soon his liver started to corrode with too much wine, his body fattened with gluttony, his senses became coarsened with the myriad pleasures of his court and his pleasure began to fade. With its gradual fading he became obsessed with the need to recreate it with ever-increasing indulgence, but his attempts were in vain. His friends, satiated with their own extravagance, left him, and in his loneliness he returned home a sadder but wiser man for he had not found happiness.

The second son decided that happiness existed not in the pursuit of pleasure but in the pursuit of power, and so he built around him a mighty army of ferocious and well-trained soldiers, hiring himself out to those who could pay him well and extend his influence. His name and that of his army became legendary for their fearsome power, and kings and princes bowed before him in the pursuit of his favour. For a while all was well and he thought he was happy, but after a while his happiness too began to fade. He real-

ized that his relationships were all based on fear. Those around him were fearful of his power and he became mistrustful of their subservience, and in doing so, turned against them. Slowly his mistrust turned into fear and then into paranoia and gradually he became transformed into a cruel and despotic tyrant. The need to protect his power dominated his thoughts and in his lonely madness he developed a terrible fear of retribution. He barricaded himself in his room at night and terrorized the world by day and eventually his tyranny created that which he feared and he was murdered.

The third son decided that the world and its temptations was the source of sorrow, and that avoidance of it would therefore be the source of happiness. And so he went off on his own into the distant hills and bought a small plot of land, some seeds and a few animals and lived as a lonely hermit, close to the soil. He subsisted on the food that his small plot of land produced, took no interest in the affairs of the little village at the foot of the hill and spent his time in quiet meditation and in prayer. For a little while all was well and he was happy in silent communion with his God and with nature. Soon, though, it became apparent that a life bereft of love and human companionship was an arid and empty dream and that a life that rejected all that gave it value and beauty was in itself a form of death. To comfort him in his solitary existence, he turned ever more fervently and hungrily to prayer and contemplation in an increasing and eventually all-consuming desire to find a full communion with his God. Gradually, he neglected his personal care and daily responsibilities and eventually his little piece of land so lovingly cared for became barren for want of maintenance, his animals grew lean and died for want of care, and he too eventually died, of hunger and madness.

The fourth son, with the example of his brothers to guide him, decided that they had failed to find happiness because they had lost their freedom of choice and had been controlled by the extremes of their nature. He decided that he would not be controlled in this way but that the principles of life would guide him on his personal path. Deciding that happiness was too elusive to follow, he defined his path as being one of duty. Duty to himself, to develop his tal-

*ents and skills, and duty to his family and community in using
those developing strengths for the benefit of those around him. In
due time, he set off for a distant village with little but his immediate needs. He worked hard to develop the basic and then specific
skills needed for survival. As he did so he developed a reputation
for thrift, endeavour and wise judgement. He eventually married
a good woman of his community and began to guide his growing
family, his friends and his community. As his reputation for wise
judgement and strength of character grew, so did his status and
influence, and after several years he became relatively important in
his local state administration. He enjoyed to the full the pleasures
that his life and status permitted, but never allowed his pursuit of
them to breach his other obligations. There were times, and as his
reputation for wise council grew, these times became more frequent,
that he was required to exercise the authority of his position both as
a parent and as a leader of his community. When he did so, however, it was always with a wise and humble caution. There were
also times however, when he retreated from the busy activity of his
community and went off on his own to the hills, sometimes for long
periods of time, to meditate in quiet community with his God, seeking guidance and strength for the challenges in the valley.*

*The fourth son soon forgot that his original quest had been
for happiness, but years later, when his father died, it was he who
became the ruler of his father's kingdom, for it was he who had
found it."*

The moral of this little story is so simple as to be obvious. Happiness does not exist in the relentless pursuit of pleasure, nor can
it be achieved under the controlling influence of power, or by
rejecting life itself. Happiness cannot be purchased, bargained
for, or even deliberately sought. Instead of passionately searching for this elusive bluebird, you should instead seek fulfilment
in your work, opportunities to develop your talents, joy in human
relationships and opportunities to serve your family and community by wise council. Only then can you achieve happiness,
not as a right, and not as a reward, but as a gift of grace.

SUMMARY OF CHAPTER TEN

1. Your attitude to life is generally directed by one of three life principles that motivate your conduct. These life principles are a desire for pleasure, a need for power and an avoidance of personal responsibility for your actions.

2. In an effective life, your actions should be generally guided by these life principles and based on their inherent usefulness as motivators to action rather than as controllers of it.

3. These three life principles, and in particular the major one that either guides you or controls you, are influenced to a great degree by your attitude to time and uncertainty and the basic trust that you have in life itself.

A FINAL WORD

In our journey together throughout this book I have stressed many times that the key to an effective life lies in the way that you interpret the events of your life and that there is an appropriate life-enhancing way of doing so. If living a full and effective life is your goal, this interpretation must be appropriate to that goal, leading, as it inevitably will, to the feelings and actions that will achieve it.

I have said that in all aspects of life there is a structured and evolving path that leads forward physically, biologically, psychologically and spiritually. In terms of its major practical application in your daily life, this means that you are led from an understanding of yourself, to an understanding of others, to an understanding of the world and finally to an understanding of life, in an expanding arena of awareness.

This understanding is initially based on a self-respect and self-love that defends your inherent value and right to exist. It develops and extends into a secure understanding of others and then into a realization that the world and the "things" in it are to be used and enjoyed as a trust and not possessively exploited. The "things" of the world include not only its material comforts, but also your personal strengths, skills, beliefs and attributes and the "attitude" you hold to their use.

This gradual integration of self, others and the world leads inevitably to a basic belief, trust and awe in the sanctity, beauty and ultimate benevolence of life itself. This does not necessarily imply a life of abundant joy or a life free from pain, but a simple acceptance of being alive with the capacity to feel both joy and pain.

Inherent in this process of growth is the optimistic belief that you can move forward into a fuller life, and that there is one into which you can move. However, optimism is a choice in which habit plays a large part. Throughout your life you build up a negative or positive personality by the way you react to both your opportunities and setbacks, and above all, by the mental habits that you have formed.

Hope, trust and optimism make life victorious, but despair, mistrust and pessimism will always defeat it. Hope integrates the body and spirit but pessimism tears them apart. Life is the battleground in which the conflict between body and spirit is waged and hope, optimism, courage and a basic love of life are the weapons with which the battle should be conducted.

Let us develop in our life a passion for whatever comes. However dark our horizons may often be, however overcast our personal skies, however rough our road, let us face life with courage, endurance and faith in our personal will. Adversity is always defeated by personal courage, obstacles will always break on the anvil of endurance and no earthly power can resist a will that is prepared to sacrifice itself in order to live. Let us take a chance on life by trusting in our own will and strength knowing that even if we are buffeted by the winds of unforeseen misfortune we would have given life itself a chance. And remember:

Be loving, for unconditional love is the doorway through which the human spirit passes from selfishness to selfhood, from solitude to kinship, and from ignorance to wisdom.

Be merciful and understanding, for these are the children of wisdom.

Be bold and confident, for magical forces wait patiently to help those who have courage and faith in their own ability.

But above all,

Smile; what sunshine is to flowers, smiles are to humanity, no power in the universe can withstand the onslaught of a well-aimed smile.

THE END

For information about Geoff Smith's work, or the intensive 4-day "New Reality" seminars and retreats which are based on this book, please contact him at:

The "New Reality" Seminars
c/o The York Learning Academy Inc.
North York Square, 45 Sheppard Avenue East,
Suite 900, North York,Ontario, Canada M2N 5W9
Email: admin@yorklearningco.ca
Tele # 905 – 886 – 4910

Or please visit:

www.newrealityseminars.ca

Further copies of this book and the authors biography are available from the publishers.

www.newrealityseminars.ca

ISBN 141208191-2

Edwards Brothers Malloy
Oxnard, CA USA
December 18, 2015